Y0-AAA-972

ECONOMIC SECURITY
IN AN
AGING POPULATION

by

Donated to
Augustana University College
by

FRANCIS   PUFFER

Butterworths
Toronto and Vancouver

Economic Security in an Aging Population
© 1991 Butterworths Canada Ltd.

All rights reserved. No part of this publication may be reproduced, stored in a retrieval system, or transmitted, in any form or by any means (photocopying, electronic, mechanical, recording, or otherwise) without the prior written permission of the copyright holder.

Grateful acknowledgement is given to the Minister of Supply and Services Canada for permission to reproduce from the Economic Council of Canada; Health and Welfare Canada; Revenue Canada Taxation; and Statistics Canada and to Doubleday Canada for *Looking After the Future* © 1987 Patrick Longhurst and Rose Marie Earle. All rights reserved.

The Butterworth Group of Companies

Canada	Butterworths Canada Ltd., 75 Clegg Road, MARKHAM, Ontario, L6G 1A1 and 409 Granville St., Ste. 1455, VANCOUVER, B.C., V6C 1T2
Australia	Butterworths Pty Ltd., SYDNEY, MELBOURNE, BRISBANE, ADELAIDE, PERTH, CANBERRA and HOBART
Ireland	Butterworths (Ireland) Ltd., DUBLIN
New Zealand	Butterworths of New Zealand Ltd., WELLINGTON and AUCKLAND
Puerto Rico	Equity de Puerto Rico, Inc., HATO REY
Singapore	Malayan Law Journal Pte. Ltd., SINGAPORE
United Kingdom	Butterworth & Co. (Publishers) Ltd., LONDON and EDINBURGH
United States	Butterworth Legal Publishers, AUSTIN, Texas; BOSTON, Massachusetts; CLEARWATER, Florida (D & S Publishers); ORFORD, New Hampshire (Equity Publishing); ST. PAUL, Minnesota; and SEATTLE, Washington

Canadian Cataloguing in Publication Data

Brown, Robert L., 1949 -
   Economic security in an Aging Population

(Perspectives on individual and population aging)
ISBN 0-409-88881-8

1. Income maintenance programs — Canada. 2. Aged — Canada — Economic conditions. 3. Economic security — Canada. I. Title. II. Series.

HD7129.B76 1990   368.4'3'00971   C90-095410-8

Sponsoring Editor - Gloria Vitale
Editor - Maura Brown
Cover Design - Patrick Ng
Production - Nancy Harding/Kevin Skinner

BUTTERWORTHS PERSPECTIVES ON INDIVIDUAL AND POPULATION AGING SERIES

This Series represents an exciting and significant development for the field of gerontology in Canada. The production of Canadian-based knowledge about individual and population aging is expanding rapidly, and students, scholars and practitioners are seeking comprehensive yet succinct summaries of the literature on specific topics. Recognizing the common need of this diverse community of gerontologists, Janet Turner, while she was Sponsoring Editor at Butterworths, conceived the idea of a series of specialized monographs that could be used in gerontology courses to complement existing texts and, at the same time, to serve as a valuable reference for those initiating research, developing policies, or providing services to elderly Canadians.

Each monograph includes a state-of-the-art review and analysis of the Canadian-based scientific and professional knowledge on the topic. Where appropriate for comparative purposes, information from other countries is introduced. In addition, some important policy and program implications of the current knowledge base are discussed, and unanswered policy and research questions are raised to stimulate further work in the area. The monographs are written for a wide audience: undergraduate students in a variety of gerontology courses; graduate students and research personnel who need a summary and analysis of the Canadian literature prior to initiating research projects; practitioners who are involved in the daily planning and delivery of services to aging adults; and policy-makers who require current and reliable information in order to design, implement and evaluate policies and legislation for an aging population.

The decision to publish a monograph on a specific topic is based in part on the relevance of the topic for the academic and professional community, as well as on the amount of information available at the time an author is signed to a contract. Because gerontology in Canada is attracting large numbers of highly qualified graduate students as well as increasingly active research personnel in academic, public and private settings, new areas of concentrated research are evolving. Future monographs will reflect this evolution of knowledge pertaining to individual or population aging in Canada.

Before introducing the tenth monograph in the Series, I would like, on

AUGUSTANA UNIVERSITY COLLEGE
LIBRARY

behalf of the Series' authors and the gerontology community, to acknowledge the following members of the Butterworths "team" and their respective staff for their unique and sincere contribution to gerontology in Canada: Andrew Martin, President, for his continuing support of the Series; Gloria Vitale, Managing Academic Editor: Acquisitions, for her enthusiastic commitment to the promotion and expansion of the Series; and Linda Kee, Executive Editor, for her co-ordination of the production, especially her constant reminders to authors (and the Series Editor) that the hands of the clock continue to move in spite of our perceptions that manuscript deadlines were still months or years away. For each of you, we hope the knowledge provided in this Series will have personal value — but not until well into the next century!

Barry D. McPherson
Series Editor

FOREWORD

One of the essential issues raised by the onset of population aging has been the necessity to provide economic security for individuals and for a society. Much of this increased interest in economic security has been initiated by unexpected advances in life expectancy and health status. But, the issue has also been raised by alarmist projections that public pension systems may become bankrupt, thereby depriving future generations of the economic support they now expect as a right because of earlier pension contributions. Furthermore, the issue is being addressed because of an increasing awareness of the diminished and disadvantaged economic status of elderly women, and because of rising health-care costs for both the individual and society. Finally, interest in this topic has been driven by a combination of tax incentives to save money for the retirement years, and by the concomitant growth of the financial planning industry. Consequently, some adults are becoming more aware of the need to plan for economic security in the later years and are demanding valid information.

Yet, despite this perception of the importance of achieving and guaranteeing economic security in later life, there is fear of the unknown, lack of knowledge and avoidance behavior on the part of the general population with respect to financial planning, Part of this unwillingness or inability to plan is related to the evolving issue of whether the responsibility for the provision of retirement income is primarily a "private trouble" or a "public issue." In reality, while income security has become a major public policy issue, in Canada and many other industrialized nations, a three-tiered system of responsibility has evolved which includes the individual, the private sector and the public sector. This monograph describes the potential contributions, as well as the advantages and disadvantages of each level of support, summarizes the public policy options related to each tier, and addresses the public policy options for providing increased economic resources to those with the lowest incomes.

Chapter 1 introduces and defines the concepts of economic "security" and "insecurity", and identifies some of the hypothesized causes of economic insecurity, including mortality, health and job loss, inflation, retirement and divorce. As the author notes, the perception or personal definition of economic security is as important as the actual economic situation. To illustrate, we have all read accounts of elderly persons who, despite living in poverty conditions, report satisfaction with their lifestyle or standard of living.

In Chapter 2 the implications for economic security of Canada's changing demographic profile is summarized, and the situation in Canada is
compared with a number of other nations. This chapter also includes an
important discussion of the policy dilemmas raised by the higher life
expectancy of females, by the increased labour force participation rates of
women, and by the greater likelihood of women living alone in the later
years because of widowhood, divorce or never marrying.

Chapter 3 outlines the sources of income available to the elderly, including cash and income-in-kind, and discusses patterns of saving *and* spending across the life cycle. Based on these analyses of income, saving and
expenditure patterns, the author illustrates the variability in the standard
of living of older Canadians and reports the prevalence of poverty and
wealth in this age group.

The next three chapters describe and analyze programs and policies
pertaining to the three major sources of retirement income. Chapter 4
presents a history and description of the various components of government-sponsored plans, including a current summary of the rules, regula-
tions and rates for contributions and payments. The chapter also introduces
a number of current public policy issues, including the mode of funding,
indexation of benefits, flexible retirement options and the principle of
universality. In Chapter 5 the history and current status of employer-
sponsored plans is described, and such issues as indexation, vesting,
portability, defined benefits vs. defined contributions, benefits at death,
mandatory retirement, employer vs. employee contributions, and tax
reform are introduced. Chapter 6 describes the history of registered retirement savings plans and illustrates their increasing importance to the
economy. In addition, this chapter addresses recent tax reforms pertaining
to pensions, and introduces the concept of reverse mortgages as a possible
source of income in the later years.

Given that increased health care costs could threaten the economic
security of an aging population, Chapter 7 describes the history of health
care funding in Canada, how the system is used and operated at present,
and how the costs in Canada compare with those in other industrialized
nations. This chapter also addresses some of the public policy issues and
needed reforms in the health care delivery system which, if implemented,
might enhance the likelihood of attaining economic security.

In order to provide a social security system that is fair, efficient and
affordable to future generations, Professor Brown introduces a number of
possible funding alternatives in Chapter 8. These options involve a consideration of fertility rates, immigration rates, rates of economic growth and
the raising of the age at which one is eligible to receive retirement benefits.

In summary, this monograph addresses important policy issues pertaining to the attainment of economic security for aging individuals and an
aging society. As such, the information will be of special interest to geron-

tology students, young adults entering the labour force, gerontologists, economists, policy-makers, financial planners and members of other professions and occupations which serve or meet the needs of adults in the pre-retirement and retirement years. The knowledge presented in this monograph should stimulate decision-makers in the public and private sectors to direct more research and policy attention to issues of aging and economic security, for both present *and* future elderly cohorts. Income security in the later years is no longer either a private trouble or a public issue. Rather, to avoid both feelings of, and states of, economic insecurity in the future, the major stakeholders — the individual, the private sector, the government — must accept a shared responsibility and initiate coordinated actions to ensure a just and sufficient income.

Barry D. McPherson, Ph.D.
Series Editor
Wilfrid Laurier University
Waterloo, Ontario, Canada
November, 1990.

PREFACE

At present, Canada has one of the youngest populations in the Western industrialized world, as measured by the percentage of the population aged 65+ to those aged 20-64. By the year 2030 (only 40 years hence) we will have one of the oldest populations, using the same measure. Hence, the consequences of an aging population are of critical importance, not only to Canada as a nation (and, thus, to its policy makers), but to all individuals in Canada.

The Series on individual and population aging initiated by Butterworths has provided a significant resource base for those seeking answers to the critical problems associated with the aging Canadian population. This monograph, *Economic Security in an Aging Population*, is another relevant building block in that foundation.

In November 1985, the Gallup organization polled over 1,000 Canadians, in a study commissioned by the Allenvest Investment Group, in an attempt to establish the views of Canadians on government-sponsored social security, employer-sponsored pension plans, and individual retirement savings programs. The results of that survey were a clear indication that Canadians knew little or nothing about the income security programs available to them.

One purpose of this monograph is to fill that void. More importantly, the monograph is a comprehensive overview of public policy in Canada in respect to the provision of economic security. Canada uses a three-tiered approach to the provision of economic security, those tiers representing the government, the employer, and the individual. Through a review of the literature, the monograph describes the evolution of the level of security provided by each sector with particular regard to why and how each sector's responsibility now exists. Finally, the monograph assumes that the provision of medical care is an essential component in the achievement of economic security. In that regard, Chapter 7 reviews the medical care delivery system and the issues around the cost of that delivery in an aging population.

The monograph opens with a philosophical discussion on what creates economic security and insecurity. This discussion shows that economic security is a very personal concept and that economic insecurity may exist through real causes or through inaccurate perceptions. The monograph's focus is to analyse sources of both security and insecurity and, for the latter, to define what is real and what is misperception.

After a description of our present demographic environment, the monograph proceeds to present a profile of the existing Canadian population aged

65 and over as to their sources of income and their expenditure and consumer habits.

The bulk of the monograph is used to present in detail the various sources of economic security available to Canadians, including those sponsored by governments, employers, and the individual. The monograph presents the advantages and disadvantages attributable to each source, and the associated future issues that may create feelings of insecurity.

Two chapters look at the future funding problems facing our health care and income security systems. The monograph closes with a chapter outlining unresolved topics and issues requiring further research.

A glossary of terms is provided for those not familiar with the income security lexicon.

It is the hope of the author that this monograph will become a permanent and regular reference for the reader.

Finally, the author wishes to thank Cathy Raithby, Fleming Armstrong, Pat Flanagan, Warren Luckner, Dr. William Forbes, and Dr. David Foot for their valuable reviews and assistance in the drafting of this document. Thanks also to Lucy Simpson for her patient and careful typing of the many drafts of the manuscript.

CONTENTS

TABLES

FIGURES

CHAPTER 1

ECONOMIC SECURITY
AND INSECURITY

1.1 INTRODUCTION

This monograph will analyse methods available to Canadians to achieve economic security. As will be seen, the present system uses a three-tiered approach to economic security, in that differing levels of support are provided by the government, the employer, and the individual. While there does exist a framework and basis for the achievement of economic security, it will be shown that Canadians are not convinced that that security exists for them, especially in the context of an aging population.

The monograph uses the opening chapter to establish a definition of economic security and insecurity. It then reviews the existing sources of economic security and analyses their respective strengths and weaknesses.

In each case, the monograph further analyses the impact that population aging will have on the system and the extent to which the aging process may create concerns about the future security of each source of benefits. In that regard, the provision of universal health care is reviewed as being an integral part of the total economic security package. It will be shown that population aging will place upward pressure on health care costs. It will be argued that, if health care costs continue to rise more rapidly than inflation, they could threaten the other government-funded (*i.e.*, tax based) sources of economic security.

Finally, the variables affecting the cost projections presented for all sources of economic security will be reviewed as to the sensitivity of the projection to each variable. Finally, public policy alternatives will be presented and analysed.

1.2 WHAT IS ECONOMIC SECURITY?

In his text, *Social Insurance and Economic Security*, Rejda (1988, 2) defines economic security as: "A state of mind or sense of well-being whereby an individual is relatively certain that he or she can satisfy basic needs and wants, both present and future." This definition of economic security is used in the discussions that follow. However, several aspects of the definition need to be highlighted.

The definition is dependent upon the individual. What provides economic security to one individual may not to another. A person who is wealthy may have different criteria for economic security than someone who is poor. Someone who grew up during the Depression may well require a higher level of proof of security before achieving a sense of well-being and satisfaction as to the future than someone from the post-war era. Hence, one's personal perception is an important part of economic security.

The definition is dynamic. Its application will vary by culture and time. Early in this century, one could achieve economic security through one's family. In an agricultural society, one's basic needs and wants could be satisfied by being part of a family unit with young members willing to provide support in one's old age. In this society, economic security was assured, as each active generation contracted to support the two adjacent dependent generations. This security could be achieved within a family unit, and society's involvement was small or non-existent. This model for the provision of economic security still exists in most developing nations.

In an industrial (or post-industrial) society, with the extended family unit no longer the norm, the above model for economic security may not work. The key to economic security in our society is income maintenance. This income must be continuous. If it is temporary, or if it can be significantly reduced, economic security will not be achieved. Thus, it is real income that matters. For example, one must be protected from the effects of inflation to feel economically secure. To know that one's future needs and wants will be satisfied requires a knowledge that the real value (purchasing power) of one's income will be maintained.

Rejda's definition of economic security requires assurance of an existence that is above an accepted definition of poverty. One must be assured of the ability to exist, not subsist. Unfortunately, it appears impossible to define these criteria objectively.

Finally, economic security is relative. As already indicated, the requirements for economic security will vary from time to time, place to place, culture to culture, and person to person. Economic security will be defined relative to the standard of living that one has grown to expect, either from one's own experience or from the experience of those around us. Hence, for an individual, there will be two key criteria for economic security. First, one must be assured of some basic level of support to satisfy the needs and wants common to all. Further, one hopes that one's standard of living will not be changed drastically by the normal events of life. Hence, a legitimate goal of a modern social security system is to provide a certain replacement ratio of previous income so as to enhance this aspect of economic security.

In this regard, it must be pointed out that one need not be poor to feel economically insecure.

As stated by the National Council of Welfare (1989b, 1):

> Canada's retirement income system is supposed to perform two essential tasks. The first is to ensure that elderly people have incomes high enough to allow them to live in dignity no matter what their circumstances were during their working years. The second is to maintain a reasonable relationship between income before and after retirement so that old age does not bring a drastic reduction in a person's standard of living.

As noted, in an agrarian society, one's needs for economic security could be and were achievable within the extended family unit, as each active generation contracted to support the two adjacent dependent generations. While this basic assumed contract is still a key ingredient, achieving full economic security cannot be and is not satisfied within each family unit. Instead, we use financial intermediaries to administer this implied contract, the most important of which is the government. The effects that an aging population will have on this new social contract will be the focus of this monograph.

1.3 WHAT IS ECONOMIC INSECURITY?

If economic security is a sense of well-being about the relative certainty of one's ability to satisfy basic needs and wants, both present and future, then economic insecurity must be a parallel sense of uncertainty. Uncertainty, in an economic sense, has been defined as an individual's subjective view of risk where risk is defined as the economic consequence of an event which can vary from the expected. Kulp and Hall (1968, 3-14) maintain that risk is objective and can be analysed mathematically (similar to statistical variance). Uncertainty, on the other hand, is subjective, and each individual can have his or her own attitudes as to the uncertainty of an event.

The chapters that follow review the sources of income maintenance available to Canadians upon retirement. Canada has a tripartite system of income maintenance in that there are three sources of income security; namely, the government, one's employer, and the individual. For any income maintenance program, one can calculate expected benefit values given certain assumptions as to rates of earnings, investment income, inflation, labour force participation, mortality, divorce, etc. However, any of these parameters can vary, for any individual, from what has been assumed. This variance attribute naturally and logically results in uncertainty for the individual, and is the source of economic insecurity. As discussed in later chapters, the fact that our population is aging (defined in Section 2.1) tends to magnify this feeling of insecurity. Two particular examples illustrate the existence of uncertainty among

Canadians. In a Gallup poll taken in November 1985 (Allenvest Group Limited 1985), Canadians were asked what created a feeling of insecurity for them. For those aged 65 and over, the items of greatest concern were disability, failure of government-sponsored income security plans, and inflation.

A second example is taken from a booklet entitled "Financial Planning for Retirement" provided by a large insurance company[1] to its employees. Under the heading "Government Programs" the booklet states: "Although we are dealing primarily with long range financial planning and since the government programs could change or not be there when you retire, we will outline at this time the present funds available from each plan and possible future availability." Later in the booklet, the various government-sponsored plans are described in more detail, but in each case the booklet indicates that there is no guarantee that the benefit will be available in the long run, and it concludes: "it is up to you to decide whether or not you include it in your retirement income plans."

Recent changes in Old Age Security benefits (see Section 4.3) as legislated by the government will reinforce the risk associated with government-sponsored social security benefits in the minds of Canadians.

1.4 CAUSES OF ECONOMIC INSECURITY

As noted in the previous section, to be able to calculate with certainty one's future income maintenance, one would need to know the exact future values of variables such as rates of earnings, investment income, inflation, labour force participation (or unemployment), mortality, divorce, etc. The following summarises some of the concerns which may in part explain one's feelings of insecurity.

Mortality

- If I die prematurely, will my dependents be economically secure?
- If I, or my spouse, live to a very old age, will our resources be exhausted?
- If my spouse dies, will I face financial difficulties?

Health

- If my health, or the health of my dependents deteriorates, what are the financial consequences to me, and to my dependents?
- Do I have sufficient resources to pay for health care costs not otherwise covered?
- Will I stay healthy enough to enjoy my retirement or should I take early retirement?

Job security

- What effect would a job change have on my income maintenance programs (*e.g.*, pension plan)?
- Could I withstand the financial consequences of an extended period of unemployment?
- What are the financial consequences of early retirement, either voluntary or forced?
- Can I withstand the job technology evolution expected during my working lifetime?

Inflation

- What effect will inflation have on the real value (purchasing power) of my income maintenance programs? Which sources are indexed to inflation — fully, partially, automatically, ad hoc?
- Do I have the financial resources to withstand a prolonged period of high rates of inflation?
- What effect will inflation have on the real value of my assets?

Retirement

- Will I have enough income from my various sources to retire in an economically secure manner?
- Will I receive the government-sponsored benefits now being promised?
- Will I be able to work after retirement should I so wish?
- What form of pay-out can I choose for my retirement income?
- What form of pay-out will optimise economic security for both me and my dependents?
- Will I be forced to retire early?

Divorce

- What are the financial implications of divorce?
- Do I have the financial resources to assure economic security if I become divorced?

This is a subjective list of questions relating to economic security. Different individuals would compile different lists and would place different emphasis on the importance of various questions.

One's attitude toward uncertainty and economic security is personal. Some people do little in the way of financial planning. In the Gallup poll previously mentioned, Canadians were asked if they had a defined system of planned savings earmarked for retirement. The survey showed that the average Canadian is not consciously planning for his or her retirement income security (48 percent of respondents reported having no retirement savings plan of any kind, nor any plan to start one).

As Schulz says in his book *The Economics of Aging*:

> The problems involved in preretirement planning are very complex. Hence, most people, having a natural inclination to live for today and avoid thinking about old age and death, give very little systematic thought to the problems until they come face to face with them — which is usually too late. The flood of criticism about the adequacy, financial inability, and equity of social security and private pensions (regardless of their merits) creates confusion and distrust among workers — further discouraging early thinking about retirement preparation (Schulz 1985, 66).

1.5 CONCLUSIONS

This chapter defined economic security, looked at reasons for one's feelings of economic insecurity, and noted the tripartite approach to providing income maintenance; namely, the government, one's employer, and the individual. It presents the philosophical theme for the remainder of the monograph; namely, what is economic security and how it can be achieved? Conversely, what is economic insecurity, and why might it exist? After a review of the existing demographics in Chapters 2 and 3, Chapters 4 through 6 then review each of the three sources of income maintenance within the environment of an aging population. Each source will be analysed as to the strengths and difficulties relevant to the perception of economic security and insecurity.

NOTE

1 Taken from *Financial Planning for Retirement*, an employee benefits booklet produced by the Co-operators Insurance Group, Guelph.

CHAPTER 2

DEMOGRAPHIC BACKGROUND

2.1 INTRODUCTION

It will be seen in later chapters that issues around population aging may be a cause of some individuals' perception of future economic insecurity. This chapter sets out to define what is meant by population aging and to explore the realities of Canada's demographic environment as a foundation for later discussion.

To understand the demographics of our population, the reader is referred to *Canada's Aging Population* by Susan McDaniel (1986), the first book in this series on individual and population aging. The summary that follows highlights those demographic factors essential to an understanding of several issues raised later. A comparison of Canadian demographics with those in other developed countries is also included.

By population aging we mean "growth over time of the proportion of old persons according to some chronological age (usually 65), in the total population" (Chen 1987). A population may "age" if individuals within the population experience enhanced life expectancy. This has been the case in Canada during this century, as the following life expectancies indicate.

TABLE 2.1

LIFE EXPECTANCY

	At Birth		At Age 65		At Age 75	
	male	female	male	female	male	female
1921	58.8	60.6	13.0	13.6	7.6	8.0
1931	60.0	62.1	13.0	13.7	7.6	8.0
1941	63.0	66.3	12.8	14.1	7.5	8.2
1951	66.3	70.8	13.3	15.0	7.9	8.8
1961	68.4	74.2	13.5	16.1	8.2	9.5
1971	69.3	76.4	13.7	17.5	8.5	10.7
1981	71.9	79.0	14.6	18.9	9.0	11.9
1986	73.0	79.7	14.9	19.1	9.1	11.9

SOURCE: Statistics Canada (Nagnur, Dhruva 1986); 1986, *Life Tables, Canada and Provinces, 1985-87.*

It is not just that elderly Canadians live longer, but also that more attain advanced ages. In 1921, 58 percent of men and 60 percent of women survived to age 65. In 1981, 75 percent of men and 86 percent of women could expect to survive from birth to age 65 (Statistics Canada: Nagnur, Dhruva 1986).

Individual aging is not the only way that the proportion of aged can increase, or a population age. Population aging, as defined, can also occur if the number of births decreases.

2.2 CANADA'S CHANGING DEMOGRAPHIC PROFILE

Figure 2.1 shows that the **fertility rates** in Canada (1901 to 1985) declined steadily and consistently from 1901 to the mid 1930s. If one were to project the trend in fertility rates in the first third of this century, one would arrive at projected rates similiar to the rates being experienced today. What is, and was, surprising, however, was the sharp rise in fertility rates in the late 1940s and 1950s, commonly referred to as the Baby Boom.

FIGURE 2.1

FERTILITY RATES

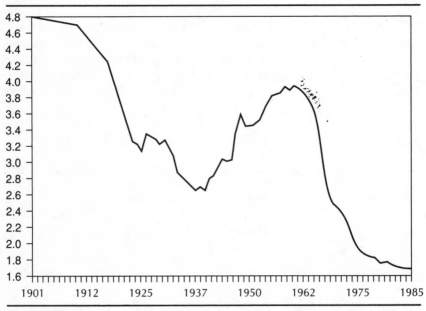

SOURCE: Statistics Canada 1984d, *Current Demographic Analysis, Fertility in Canada*, Catalogue 91-524E, 121-22.

Figure 2.2 presents a slightly different picture of the same demographic phenomenon.

FIGURE 2.2

NUMBER OF LIVE BIRTHS

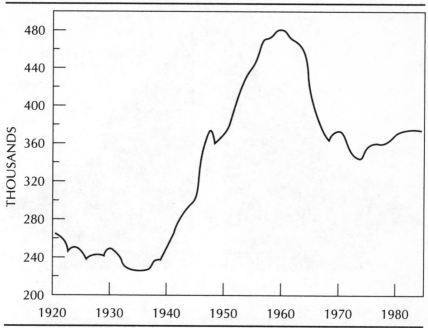

SOURCE: Statistics Canada, *Current Demographic Analysis, Fertility in Canada*, Catalogue 91-524E, 121-22.

In this monograph, any reference to the Baby Boom implies the population born in the fourteen-year period from 1952 to 1965, inclusive, the only years when live births exceeded 400,000 per annum. While this definition may seem arbitrary, it lends itself to a logical explanation of many of the funding controversies that will be discussed later, and it is also a definition used by others (*e.g.*, Kettle 1980).

At the end of 1965, one-third of Canada's population was 0 to 14, *i.e.*, they were members of the Baby Boom. Also, despite a significantly increased population base, the number of live births in 1987 was still not as great as during any of the Baby Boom years. In 1965, Canada had a "young" population, with only 7.7 percent of the population aged 65 and over.

What followed the Baby Boom was the equally important Baby Bust. The demographic effect of the Baby-Boom-Baby-Bust wave is illustrated in Figure 2.3.

FIGURE 2.3*
POPULATION PYRAMIDS
1981, 2001, 2051

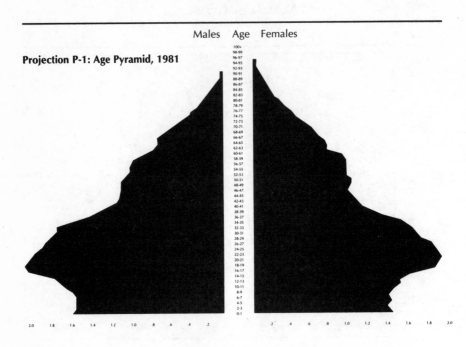

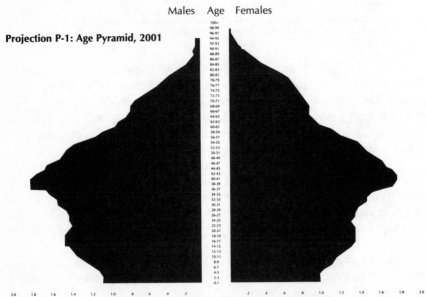

FIGURE 2.3*, cont'd
POPULATION PYRAMIDS
1981, 2001, 2051

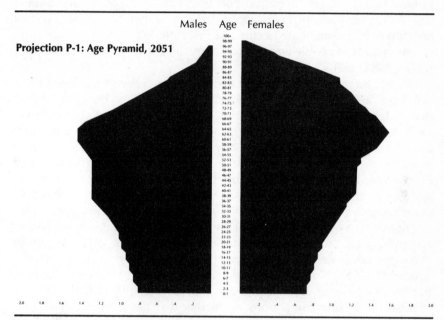

NOTE: The horizontal scale indicates percent of total population.
         *Assumes that the fertility rate decreases linearly from 1.7 to 1.4 by 1996 and then remains
         level.
SOURCE: Marshall 1987, 28-32.

As previously noted, the percentage of the population aged 65 and over
in 1965 was 7.7 percent. By 2005, it is estimated that this figure will be 12.5
percent, and by 2025, 18.8 percent (see Table 2.2) under medium-variant
data generated by the U.N. Population division 1984 (U.S. Department of
Commerce 1987, 71).

2.3 THE IMPACT OF THE SHIFTING DEMOGRAPHICS

On a macro, or total, population basis, the decline in birth rates and
enhanced life expectancy means that Canada will have fewer young
people to provide economic security for a larger number of the elderly.
This is also true on an individual basis. Where there used to be several
children in a family to share the care of one set of parents, there are now
only one or two. Preston (1984, 44-49) points out that this is the first time
in history that the average married couple has more parents than children.

"If the 1980 rates of fertility and mortality persist, a forty-year-old couple in 2020 can expect to have 2.88 living parents and 1.78 living children" (Pifer and Bronte 1986, 166).

The increase in life expectancy in this century has created a new demographic reality: "...we have almost become a different species. Retirement used to be rare, because most people died during their work lives. At least one parent had usually died before the last child left home. Orphans were common and old people were scarce. Now the opposite is true" (Pifer and Bronte 1986, 267).

Despite these rapid shifts, older people have not been abandoned by or isolated from their families. The elderly were not treated better in the past than today, nor better in less complex societies than in our own (Marshall 1987, 311). The family continues to be a vital part in the lives of older Canadians. However, we cannot rely on the family as the sole support basis for the elderly. To do so would ignore the growing minority of elderly who have no children." About 10 percent of women never marry and 14 percent have no children, so that about 18 percent or so of people over the age of 65 are found to have no children alive" (Marshall 1987, 478).

There is no reason to believe that the decline in fertility will end. Women are continuing to have their first child at older ages, and the rate of marriage continues to decline (Statistics Canada, Current Demographic Analysis 1986b). While the decline in fertility rates has slowed, Canada's fertility rates (except perhaps in Quebec) are still significantly above those of most West European nations, so further declines are possible.

Another reason for the elderly living alone is divorce. From 1969-1983 there was uninterrupted growth in both absolute numbers and rates of divorce, which then levelled off (Statistics Canada 1986b). A further relaxation of divorce laws in 1985 has led to a further increase (which may prove to be only temporary). A total of 86,985 divorces were granted in 1987, 40 percent more than in 1985.

Many aging societies are characterized as divorcing societies. As Pifer and Bronte (1986, 152) note:

> The historian Philippe Ariès has suggested that this may be inevitable, because modern longevity makes marriage a much more long-term commitment than it was in the past. At the end of the nineteenth century, the average length of marriage until the time when one's spouse died was about twenty-eight years. In the late 1970s it was over forty-three years. In the typical nineteenth-century family, one spouse was deceased before all the children were raised.

Marital disruption and remarriage have existed throughout history; the only notable change is that the cause of disruption is now commonly divorce, not death. These high divorce rates may result in more elderly individuals looking to society for their health and social-support services (for an in-depth discussion, see Connidis 1989 33-37). Also, older people in general do not wish to rely on their children for health and social-support services (Marshall 1987, 478).

In analysing the effects of the shifting demographics in later chapters, we will be concerned, not only with the growth in the proportion of those aged 65 and over, but also with the expected growth of those aged 75 and over or 80 and over.

The major problems of health and security will shift to the very old, those 80 and older. By 2025, they will account for 5 percent of the population, and two-thirds of them will be women (Health and Welfare Canada 1987b, 8).

Those 75 years and older accounted for 31 percent of the elderly population in 1951 and rose to 37 percent in 1981. By 2031, when the aged population "explosion" as a result of the "baby boom bulge" materializes, it is projected that those aged 75 and older will comprise 45 to 50 percent of the elderly population (Simmons-Tropea *et. al.* 1986, 4).

This has an important impact on the funding requirements of both health and social security programs as will be seen in later chapters.

2.4 AN INTERNATIONAL COMPARISON

Table 2.2 presents an international comparison of aging populations.

TABLE 2.2
AGED POPULATION RATIOS (%)

Country	1985			2005			2025		
%	65+	75+	85+	65+	75+	85+	65+	75+	85+
France	12.4	6.2	3.2	14.8	6.4	3.1	19.3	7.9	3.8
W. Germ	14.5	6.8	3.2	18.9	7.5	3.8	22.5	9.5	5.3
Italy	13.0	5.5	2.5	16.9	7.0	3.4	19.6	8.6	4.3
U.K.	15.1	6.3	3.1	15.3	6.9	3.8	18.7	8.1	4.0
Sweden	16.9	7.2	3.5	17.2	8.2	4.7	22.2	10.5	5.2
U.S.	12.0	4.9	2.6	13.1	6.7	4.1	19.5	8.5	4.8
Canada	10.4	4.0	2.0	12.5	5.6	3.0	18.8	7.5	3.7
Australia	10.1	3.7	1.7	11.4	4.8	2.4	15.9	6.2	2.9
Japan	10.0	3.7	1.7	16.5	6.4	3.0	20.3	10.0	4.9
China	5.1	1.4	0.5	7.4	2.4	1.0	12.8	4.1	1.8
Hong Kong	7.6	2.4	1.0	10.3	4.3	2.1	17.5	5.8	2.6
India	4.3	1.1	0.4	6.1	1.8	0.7	9.7	3.1	1.3
Israel	8.9	3.6	1.5	8.3	3.5	1.8	11.9	4.7	2.1

SOURCE: U.S. Department of Commerce 1987, 46-62.

From this table, one can see that Canada at present has a relatively "young" population when compared with the rest of the industrialized world. Sweden is currently the "oldest" country in the world, with about 17 percent of its population aged 65 and over (more than one in six). By contrast, Canada has only about one in ten aged 65 and over.

The aging of the population over the next forty years will not be at a constant rate. "For most countries listed, there will be modest increases in the size of the elderly population relative to the size of the working-age population over the next 20 years, but sharp increases from 2005 to 2025" (U.S. Department of Commerce 1987, vii).

In terms of the ability of governments to enact public policy change, it is not just the level of the population of elderly dependents that will be important, but also the rate at which that proportion will change (see Table 2.3).

TABLE 2.3

PROJECTED PERCENT INCREASE IN THE POPULATION 65+: 1985 TO 2025

Country	% Increase
India	264
China	238
Hong Kong	219
Canada	135
Australia	125
Japan	121
Israel	116
U.S.	105
France	67
Italy	51
W. Germany	36
U.K.	23
Sweden	21

SOURCE: U.S. Department of Commerce 1987, 6.

For example, while Sweden today has the world's "oldest" population, public policy shifts over the next forty years may be relatively easy, as they anticipate only a 21 percent growth in their elderly population. Hence, Sweden will not face significant shifts in the distribution of wealth in the next forty years because of population aging.

In Canada, however, the number of elderly will grow more than 135 percent, with most of that growth being experienced after 2010. Hence, without proper planning, required public policy shifts may be too rapid and dramatic to occur without voter dissatisfaction (see Chapters 7 and 8).

2.5 THE CASE OF WOMEN

In any discussion of population aging, women require special attention.

Elderly women greatly outnumber elderly men in most countries of the world. Therefore, the social, economic, and health problems of the elderly are in large part the problems of elderly women. Not only do women have higher life expectancies at birth, but female death rates are lower than male death rates at all ages in virtually all countries. Consequently, as a population ages, the percentage of women in each age cohort steadily increases. This trend is especially pronounced in developed countries, where the proportion of women among the oldest old reaches as high as 70 percent (U.S. Department of Commerce 1987, 21).

Table 2.1 shows that female life expectancy in Canada exceeds male life expectancy at all ages listed. In fact, the improvement in female life expectancy exceeded the improvement in male life expectancy until 1981, when the trend reversed. As yet, it is not clear what caused this reversal, but Wigdor and Foot (1988, 70) offer one explanation: "Men are showing a decline in death rate from heart disease and cancer particularly because they are smoking and drinking less, while women seem to be showing the effects of continued smoking, and what is considered increased stress due to multiple roles of worker and homemaker."

The higher life expectancy of women presents several policy dilemmas. For example, inflation protection is more important to an elderly woman than to an elderly man. Given a life expectancy of 19.1 years at age 65 and an inflation rate of only 3.7 percent, well below rates experienced today, a Canadian woman on fixed income would see the purchasing power of that income cut in half during her expected lifetime.

Elderly women are more apt to live alone. In Canada, over one-fourth of the elderly and a third of those 75 and over live by themselves. Within the former group, 36 percent of women versus 14 percent of men live alone; the figures for those 75 and over are 45 and 19 percent, respectively. The ratio of elderly women to men in Canada is 1.3 to 1; the ratio living alone is 3.3 to 1 (U.S. Department of Commerce 1987, 29).

We see a similar disparity of statistics with respect to widowhood (see Table 2.4).

TABLE 2.4

PERCENTAGE OF WIDOWED INDIVIDUALS

Age	Females	Males
55-64	16.7	3.3
65-74	37.0	8.4
75+	66.9	25.4

SOURCE: Statistics Canada 1982, *Census of Canada 1981 Population*, Catalogue 92-901.

The relatively high proportion of widows to widowers can be explained by three factors:

(i)   longer life expectancy of women;
(ii) the general tendency of the male spouse to be older than the female spouse;
(iii) the greater likelihood of men to remarry.

For those aged 65 and over in 1986, 77 percent of men were married versus 41 percent for women (Connidis 1989, 9).

Remarriage is becoming a male experience, especially at advanced ages (see Table 2.5).

TABLE 2.5

AGE -SPECIFIC REMARRIAGE RATES (PER 1000)
WIDOWERS AND WIDOWS
CANADA 1981

Age	Widowers	Widows
60-64	43.6	7.8
65-69	33.8	5.0
70-74	22.4	2.8
75+	6.7	0.7

SOURCE: Connidis 1989, 35.

A spouse is one of the most important resources for an older person. The fact that many elderly women live alone must be addressed in any public policy alternatives.

Finally, the rapid entry of women into the labour force during the past twenty years has changed the Canadian labour profile. This has already resulted in increased pressure on the government for more child care facilities and may translate into increased demands for expanded elderly care facilities if women are forced to abandon or curtail their traditional roles as caregivers. Figure 2.4 presents the rise in female labour force participation rates juxtaposed with the drop in total fertility rates.

In 1966, the female labour force participation rate was 35.4 percent. By 1987, it was 56.2 percent. Conversely in 1966, the total fertility rate was 2.812, but by 1987 it was 1.665. In the period 1981-86, women accounted for 75 percent of the growth in the labour force and 94 percent of the additional jobs.

The entry of women into the labour force has both positive and negative funding implications that we will explore later. On the positive side, the funding of social security (*e.g.,* the Canada Pension Plan) has been

FIGURE 2.4

FEMALE LABOUR FORCE PARTICIPATION RATES
VERSUS
TOTAL FERTILITY RATES

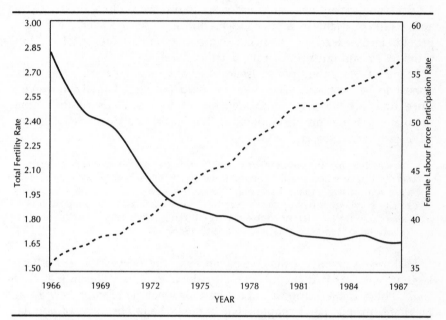

SOURCE:Statistics Canada 1988a, *Historical Labour Force Statistics*, Catalogue 71-201, 240-56; Statistics Canada 1984d, *Current Demographic Analysis, Fertility in Canada*, Catalogue 91-524E, 121, 122.

enhanced by the entry of these new worker-participants (see Fellegi 1988, 4.1). On the other hand, the entry of middle-aged women into the paid labour force may decrease their ability to provide care to older family members. This may mean that such elderly dependents must rely on government-subsidized care to a greater extent.

As Canadians have moved from an agrarian society, through an industrial, to a post-industrial society, government has been called upon to provide many of the services required by the elderly that were previously the responsibility of the extended family. Examples are meals-on-wheels and home-care services. When the government accepted this responsibility, it also became accepted that children were no longer necessary to provide us with economic security in old age. However, with the decline in birth rates, there may now be the perception that there will be too few workers in the next century to provide economic security to the rapidly rising number of elderly (see Section 8.2).

2.6 CONCLUSIONS

Figure 2.3 illustrates the demographic shifts resulting from increased life expectancies and declining birth rates. Improved mortality means that increasing numbers of people will survive to retirement and will spend an extended period of time in retirement. This is a recent phenomenon. To date, our society has not found ways to use the skills of these elderly and refers to them as a "dependent burden." As a society, we have provided considerable resources to prolong human life but have not provided meaningful social roles for the elderly.

Many of the public policy issues relevant to population aging may appear to be problems. The elderly should not be "blamed," however, since they are simply the messengers of future needs of the aging population. For example, separating the elderly as dependents is not advised in the research.

> . . . if we ghettoize the old in institutions, high-rise apartments for the elderly and the like, we necessarily ghettoize the young elsewhere. If we continue to use seniority as a major basis of job protection and remuneration, we necessarily privilege the old over the young. If we target social services on the basis of age rather than need, we risk reinforcing negatively consequential stereotypes of the aged (Statistics Canada 1986b, 1).

Historically, many of the consequences of the Baby Boom have been largely unanticipated in public policy debates (see, for example, Foot 1982). Policy makers appear unprepared for what demographers view as inevitable events. Later chapters will explore the implications of population aging and the effect it may have on one's feeling of economic security, both real and perceived. First, however, we will look at the income and expenditure patterns of our present elderly population.

CHAPTER 3

INCOME AND EXPENDITURE PATTERNS OF THE ELDERLY IN CANADA

3.1 INTRODUCTION

This chapter discusses the sources of income to the elderly, both cash income and income-in-kind (*e.g.*, free prescription drugs). It then looks at consumption patterns and compares the consumption patterns of the elderly with those of other Canadians. It also analyses the effect population aging is expected to have on total savings. Further, it discusses the prevalence of poverty and wealth among the elderly.

In Chapter 1, it was noted that economic security requires both a basic level of income and some continuation of one's standard of living. With that in mind, this chapter will also discuss income replacement ratios at retirement.

3.2 SOURCES OF INCOME

Table 3.1 compares sources of income for persons 65 years and over in 1971 and 1985.

TABLE 3.1

PERCENTAGE OF INCOME FROM VARIOUS SOURCES FOR PERSONS 65 YEARS AND OVER

	1971		1985	
	Male	Female	Male	Female
	%	%	%	%
Private Pension	16.5	8.6	20.5	9.0
C/QPP	2.2	1.1	15.5	10.1
OAS/GIS	29.3	60.5	26.1	45.2
Investment Income	20.5	19.7	21.2	28.0
Other Income	31.6	10.1	16.8	7.8
	100.0	100.0	100.0	100.0

SOURCE: Statistics Canada 1988b, 97, 105.

Table 3.1 shows a remarkable change in income sources during the four-teen-year period. The proportion of income denoted "other" (which includes earnings) has decreased, while the proportion of income from the Canada/Quebec Pension Plan (C/QPP) has increased significantly. In fact, the C/QPP was an insignificant source of income for both women and men in 1971, primarily because the C/QPP plan was not introduced until 1966 and did not pay full benefits until 1976. Hence, in 1971, few Canadians aged 65 and over were receiving C/QPP retirement benefits, and those that were, were only receiving partial (immature) benefits (at most, half of the full benefit level). Also, women appear to be less dependent on income from the Guaranteed Income Supplement (GIS).

As the C/QPP matures, we can expect the importance of C/QPP income to continue to rise, especially for women, because of their increased presence in the labour force. C/QPP benefits are earnings related (see Section 4.6), so that women who have not been in the work force do not earn C/QPP credits. Any benefits they receive will be as survivors of working spouses who have C/QPP benefits (see Section 4.6). However, because of the increased female labour force participation rates, women will now accrue their own C/QPP credits. The historic progress of women as contributors to the C/QPP is shown in Table 3.2.

TABLE 3.2

C/QPP CONTRIBUTORS BY SEX
(AS A % OF THOSE AGED 20-64)

Year	Women	Men
1971	53.1	97.4
1976	55.6	95.6
1981	62.7	91.3

SOURCE: National Council of Welfare 1984b, 36.

The percentage of women contributing to the C/QPP is expected to continue to rise. According to the Economic Council of Canada, the proportion of women aged 65 and over who will *not* be beneficiaries of their own C/QPP retirement pension (as opposed to only the reduced survivor's pension) will decrease from 68 percent in 1981 to 12 percent by the year 2031 (Economic Council of Canada 1979, 108).

In its analysis, *One in Three — Pensions for Canadians to 2030*, the Economic Council of Canada (1979, 38) suggested that an amendment to the Canada Pension Plan allowing a child-rearing dropout period would produce about 22 percent higher retirement benefits for the average mother. Such an amendment was passed in 1977 for the Quebec Pension Plan and in 1983 for the Canada Pension Plan.

One can also see improved income from private source pensions, annuities, and other income, because more Canadians are being covered by private pensions or RRSPs (see Chapters 5 and 6). Recent pension reform legislation and increased tax incentives for RRSPs should mean that the growth in private source retirement income will continue.

Historically, relatively few women have earned benefits from private pension plans as wage earners. Lack of coverage for part-time workers and long vesting periods (the length of period of employment required to gain rights to the employer's contributions) have resulted in women obtaining minimal retirement incomes. Further, relatively few widows received survivor's benefits from their husband's private pension plans. All three of these issues have been addressed by pension reform legislation (see Section 5.5).

However, as long as women participate in the work force to a lesser extent than men, earn lower wages than men, and hold more part-time jobs (25 percent of women work part-time, versus 8 percent of men), retirement income for women will not be as large as for men (Economic Council of Canada 1979, 35).

It is also informative to compare income sources by age. The relative importance of certain income sources for the active work force versus the elderly can also be compared, as well as sources of income for the young-old versus the old-old (see Table 3.3).

Sources of income vary significantly by age, but an examination based on cross-sectional data, *i.e.*, data on income and expenditures for different age groups at one point in time, magnifies the inequalities existing between the population groups at that time. These inequalities may spring from characteristics particular to that age group. For example, those 80+ receive a much smaller portion of their income from C/QPP benefits, because the C/QPP retirement income benefits did not reach their full benefit level until 1976. Hence, anyone now 80+ will be receiving small or no C/QPP retirement income benefits, which will not be true for this same age group in another twenty years. It may therefore be desirable to present information like that in Table 3.3 in the form of a cohort analysis, which traces the development of one group's (*e.g.*, the cohort defined by year of birth) income and expenditure through time. Such a presentation is reviewed later, in Table 3.8.

Income sources also vary from province to province, especially for the aged poor. Six provinces and the two territories provide supplements over and above the federal Guaranteed Income Supplement (GIS) (see Appendix). The other four provinces do not. This source of income explains much of the difference between Table 3.3, column 7, Government Transfers Total, and the sum of columns 5 (OAS/GIS) and 6 (C/QPP).

TABLE 3.3

MAJOR INCOME COMPONENTS FOR FAMILIES AND UNATTACHED
INDIVIDUALS, BY AGE OF HEAD, CANADA 1983
(PERCENTAGE DISTRIBUTION)

	Earnings			Investment Income	Government Transfers			Retirement Pensions	Total Income
Age of Head	Wages & Salaries	Self-Employ	Total		OAS/GIS Benefits	CPP/QPP Benefits	Total		
	All Families and Unattached Individuals								
50-54	80.5	5.8	86.3	5.5	0.4	0.4	6.4	0.8	100.0
55-59	73.4	6.8	80.2	8.7	0.4	1.0	7.2	2.8	100.0
60-64	62.0	6.2	68.1	11.4	1.3	2.0	10.5	8.2	100.0
65-69	29.2	4.0	33.3	16.6	20.5	10.5	35.5	12.5	100.0
70-74	16.8	3.1	19.9	21.4	30.6	12.8	47.0	10.7	100.0
75-79	10.4	2.8	13.3	23.0	37.2	9.9	50.3	12.2	100.0
80+	7.5	0.8	8.3	25.1	44.8	4.9	55.6	9.9	100.0
	Families with Head and Spouse Present								
50-54	81.6	6.5	88.0	5.6	0.3	0.2	5.1	0.6	100.0
55-59	76.3	7.2	83.5	7.8	0.3	0.5	5.7	2.1	100.0
60-64	64.2	6.8	71.0	10.7	1.2	1.2	8.5	8.2	100.0
65-69	32.9	4.6	37.5	15.9	18.4	9.9	32.3	12.2	100.0
70-74	17.3	4.2	21.4	22.0	28.0	12.6	43.8	11.7	100.0
75-79	11.5	3.2	14.7	21.2	36.3	10.0	49.0	13.6	100.0
80+	4.5	0.5	5.0	28.3	44.0	6.1	54.4	11.6	100.0

NOTE: Components may not sum to totals because of rounding and because not all components
are shown.
SOURCE: Task Force on Inflation Protection, Vol. 1 1988, 239.

It should also be noted that the incomes of the elderly have increased
considerably, relative to the rest of the Canadian population, since 1960.
In 1960, the average income of individuals 65 and over was one-half the
average income of all individuals. By 1984, the average income of
individuals aged 65 and over was nearly three-quarters of the average
income of all Canadian individuals (International Social Security Association 1987, 116).

3.3 INCOME-IN-KIND

The elderly also receive other benefits which are not paid in cash. We will
refer to these as "income-in-kind." Table 3.4 lists the benefits available to

TABLE 3.4

GAINS-A BENEFITS — INCOME GUARANTEE
BENEFIT LEVELS OCTOBER TO DECEMBER 1989

	OAS/GIS/Gains-A Benefits			
	Single		**Couple**	
Income	**Monthly**	**Yearly**	**Monthly**	**Yearly**
OAS	$337.04	$4,044.48	$674.08	$8,088.96
GIS	400.53	4,806.36	521.76	6,261.12
Gains-A-Max*	83.00	996.00	166.00	1,992.00
Sub-Total	$820.57	$9,846.84	$1,361.84	$16,342.08
	Additional Benefits			
Drug Benefit		$548.00		$1,096.00
OHIP Prem. Waiver		$357.96		$715.92
Sales Tax Grant		$50.00		$100.00
Property Tax Grant		Up to $600.00		Up to $600.00
Sub Total		$1,555.96		$2,511.92
Total		$11,402.80		$18,854.00
Statistics Canada Low-Income Cutoffs				
Low-End (Rural Communities)		$8,555.00		$11,181.00
High-End (Large Metropolitan Centres)		$11,569.00		$15,263.00

* Gains-A: Province of Ontario's Guaranteed Annual Income System

SOURCE: Province of Ontario, Senior Citizens Information Centre.

either an individual or a couple living in the province of Ontario in the last quarter of 1989 when there is no personal source of income, including CPP income.

Of the $11,402.80 available to a single person, 14 percent comes from non-cash benefits, *i.e.*, those listed as "Additional Benefits." Similarly, for a couple, 13 percent of the total benefit is "income-in-kind." Other examples of provincial non-cash benefits to the elderly are summarized in the Appendix to this chapter.

Also, Canadians benefit from a health care system funded from general tax revenues. It has been estimated that the incomes of elderly Canadians would have to be as much as one-third higher if they had to pay for the various services covered under public health insurance (National Council of Welfare 1984a, 62).

The elderly also have several age-related tax advantages that enhance their after-tax income, which is the proper indication of purchasing power or wealth. Two tax advantages, the sales tax grant and the property tax grant, are listed in Table 3.4 and vary from province to province. There are several other tax concessions for seniors. First is the age exemption, which reduces the taxable income of elderly taxpayers (by $2,640 in 1987). Because this deduction from taxable income is worth more to the wealthy (as much as $1,320) and is worth nothing to someone receiving only OAS and GIS, it was changed to a tax credit, worth $550, in 1988. The cost of the age exemption, in lost tax revenue, in 1984 to the federal and provincial governments was approximately $620 million dollars (McDonald 1985).

A second tax measure, the pension income deduction, exempts from tax $1,000 of private pension income. Again, because this is of no benefit to those who are without such pension income, or are too poor to pay income tax, it has also been converted to a tax credit, worth $170, in 1988. The cost, in lost tax revenue, in 1984 of the $1,000 pension income exemption was estimated to be $350 million dollars (McDonald 1985).

Moreover, price reductions and various subsidies are widely available to persons aged 65 and over, and in some cases to persons as young as 55. These include retail discounts (*e.g.*, senior citizen discount shopping days), subsidies for transportation, and a variety of other income-in-kind transactions.

Retired people also have more time available to do "home production." While the value of this time may be low per hour, its total value can be considerable, and it is not counted as part of measured income (Task Force on Inflation Protection, Vol. 1. 1988, 249). Later chapters will also review the importance of the health, recreational, and personal care made available by friends and relatives.

Finally, an important part of income security for the elderly is home ownership. This aspect of wealth is not reflected in the income statistics, nor is it reflected in the needs test required for income supplementation (which are income based — see Sections 4.4 and 4.5), even though home ownership contributes to economic security (see Section 3.7).

3.4 CONSUMPTION PATTERNS

Table 3.5 presents data on consumption patterns for families in Ontario. Other data (*e.g.*, Marr and McCready 1989, 106) show that these Ontario patterns of consumption reflect Canada-wide patterns.

Table 3.5 shows that average consumption expenditure rises with age, to age group 45 to 49, and then declines for each subsequent age group. It can be shown (Task Force on Inflation Protection, Vol. 1 1988, 249) that this decline in consumption mirrors the decline of average income. Family units, over the ages analysed, spend less than their current income on consumption. Even people age 75 and over appear to continue to accumulate assets rather than spend their income on current consumption

TABLE 3.5

DISTRIBUTION OF CONSUMPTION EXPENDITURES BY AGE OF HEAD AND EXPENDITURE CATEGORY, ONTARIO 1982 (PERCENTAGES) (DOLLAR AVERAGE IN BRACKETS)

Category	All Ages	25-29	35-39	45-49	55-59	60-64	65-69	70-74	75+
Food	21.3	19.0	20.8	22.0	22.9	23.2	23.5	23.9	24.8
	(4,218)	(3,673)	(4,969)	(5,648)	(4,515)	(3,718)	(3,132)	(2,739)	(2,289)
Purchased	16.2	12.9	15.8	17.1	18.2	19.0	19.4	20.1	21.6
from stores	(3,207)	(2,496)	(3,773)	(4,385)	(3,590)	(3,048)	(2,589)	(2,298)	(1,993)
Purchased	5.0	6.0	5.0	4.9	4.6	4.1	4.0	3.7	2.7
from	(995)	(1,164)	(1,188)	(1,253)	(915)	(660)	(526)	(429)	(248)
Restaurants									
Housing	36.1	38.5	38.2	32.5	31.6	33.9	36.9	39.6	45.4
	(7,160)	(7,444)	(9,111)	(8,331)	(6,247)	(5,432)	(4,917)	(4,534)	(4,192)
Clothing	8.8	8.2	8.8	10.0	8.7	8.2	7.3	6.3	6.5
	(1,738)	(1,585)	(2,095)	(2,564)	(1,719)	(1,315)	(976)	(726)	(698)
Transportation	16.4	16.3	15.4	16.7	18.6	19.1	16.2	16.5	10.7
	(3,241)	(3,151)	(3,679)	(4,278)	(3,678)	(3,061)	(2,162)	(1,889)	(984)
Health and	4.3	3.9	4.1	4.7	4.6	4.5	4.9	4.7	5.1
Personal Care	(855)	(752)	(983)	(1,210)	(904)	(719)	(650)	(544)	(474)
Recreation,	8.4	8.7	8.6	9.5	8.2	6.5	6.6	5.8	4.9
Reading and	(1,672)	(1,679)	(2,045)	(2,436)	(1,617)	(1,043)	(880)	(663)	(456)
Education									
Tobacco and	4.7	5.4	4.2	4.5	5.4	4.7	4.5	3.2	2.5
Alcohol	(932)	(1,041)	(998)	(1,164)	(1,066)	(756)	(594)	(364)	(234)
Total	100.0	100.0	100.0	100.0	100.0	100.0	100.0	100.0	100.0
Expenditure	(19,817)	(19,326)	(23,879)	(25,633)	(19,746)	(16,044)	(13,311)	(11,459)	(9,226)

NOTE: Components may not sum exactly to totals because of rounding error.
SOURCE: Task Force on Inflation Protection, Vol. 1 1988, 255, 256.

(Task Force on Inflation Protection, Vol. 1 1988, 249; Foot and Trefler 1983). Food and housing, the two leading categories, account for over half of all expenditures in all age groups. The percentage of an individual's budget spent on food rises with age, while restaurant expenditures fall. The percentage spent on housing (shelter, household operation, and household furnishings and equipment) declines up to age 55 to 59, but then rises sharply for the older age groups. For those aged 75 and over, 70 percent of the budget is spent on food and housing. Thus, factors affecting the price of food and shelter will impact heavily on the elderly. The Task Force on Inflation Protection (Vol. 1 1988, 253) also reanalysed these patterns while adjusting to control for the effects of cross-variables such as spending unit size (*e.g.*, one or two persons), income level, education of head, and so on. They showed that the effects of age alone are less pronounced than one would have concluded, based on Table 3.5 alone.

The Task Force also concluded that for spending units with heads aged 75 and over, there is evidence that average expenditure levels for this age group decline, when compared with younger age groups, even if these incomes were not lower. However, it is not possible (because of a lack of information on health status) to know whether such reduced consumption levels are due to poorer average health, and the resultant curtailment of certain activities (Task Force on Inflation Protection, Vol. 1 1988, 289).

3.5 SAVINGS

There exists a myth that savings patterns follow a well-defined life cycle. Young workers and families go into debt as they acquire homes and furnishings. With time, they pay off their debt and become net savers. Then they "dis-save" in retirement as they live off their accumulated wealth. Hence, we would expect individual savings to peak at the time of retirement.

Empirical evidence suggests otherwise. Foot and Trefler (1983, 11) determined that, while real per family net income peaks at a slightly later age than consumption; namely, around age 44, net savings peak much later. Because total consumption declines at a faster rate than income, per family savings does not peak until age 52.5 years. What is more important, especially for public policy analysis, is that savings remain positive throughout the later years of the life cycle. Since income in this period is falling, the savings *rate* does not peak until age 67 (see Figure 3.1).

Foot and Trefler (1983) conclude that an aging population may generate more total savings and, therefore, more capacity for economic growth. This conclusion is in contrast to that reached by others, who believe that high levels of aged dependency impose a constraint on the potential for saving and growth (see, for example, Soderstrom 1982).

3.6 THE PREVALENCE OF POVERTY

The material presented to this point outlined several factors that indicate that our society is providing significant economic security for the elderly in Canada. For example, Canadians are able to continue to save even after retirement. The implementation of the C/QPP and the improved security indicated by pension reform legislation (see Section 5.5) have enhanced financial security. Also, as noted, the elderly have significant non-money

FIGURE 3.1
SAVINGS RATES 1964-1978

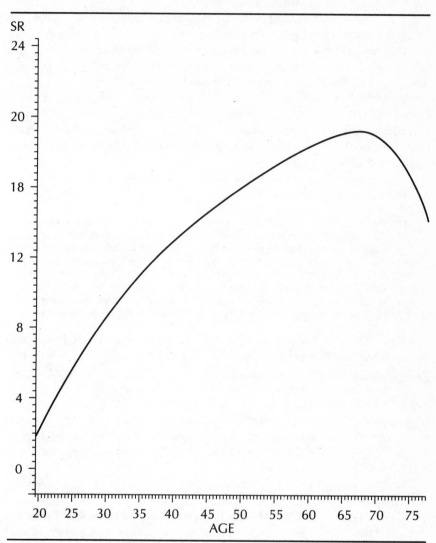

SOURCE: Foot and Trefler 1983, 15.

sources of financial security (income-in-kind).

Statistics from the National Council of Welfare (1988) indicate a continuation of poverty for many, however. This agency defines the Canadian poverty line as the income level where, on average, 58.5 percent of income is used for the essentials of life. This is based on gross rather than net (after-tax) income and is 20 percentage points above the average. These lines correspond to Statistics Canada "low-income cutoffs" used to define the low-income population.

While some feel that the Statistics Canada criterion results in an excessive indication of poverty, measures used by other agencies produce even higher poverty lines. For 1986, the most recent year for which data are available, 3,689,000 Canadians, or one in seven, lived below the poverty line as just defined. Over one million of these are children.

Unattached elderly Canadians (*i.e.*, those who live alone or in a household where they are not related to other members) are the next largest identifiable group living in poverty. In 1986, 42.7 percent, or 336,000, were below the poverty line. The poverty ratio is even higher (46.1 percent) for unattached elderly women.

These figures still represent a significant improvement in the fight against poverty.

In 1980, 61.5 percent of unattached seniors were below the poverty line. By 1986, 42.7 percent had low incomes — still high, but much better than at the beginning of the decade. The poverty rate for families with heads 65 or older declined from 41.4 percent in 1969 to 14.2 percent in 1980 and just 9.5 percent in 1986. Improvements in the retirement income system, such as the federal Guaranteed Income Supplement for the low-income elderly and the maturation of the Canada and Quebec Pension Plans, largely take the credit for fighting poverty among the aged (National Council of Welfare 1988, 1).

Elderly families (those 65+), where 9.5 percent are considered poor, can be considered better off than those in the 60 to 64 category, where 11.0 percent are listed as poor. Also, the poverty ratio for elderly families is lower than that for families led by persons under age 65 — 9.5 percent versus 12.8 percent (National Council of Welfare 1988, 35).

As noted, 46.1 percent of unattached elderly women can be considered to be poor. Also, 23.5 percent of elderly women can be considered as poor versus 12.5 percent of elderly men. Overall, 71.7 percent of all seniors below the poverty line are women.

While these figures are of concern, they do show some improvement from historical data. In 1980, 65.4 percent of unattached women were poor, versus 46.1 percent in 1986. The poverty ratio for aged unattached men fell from 51.9 percent in 1980 to 31.9 percent in 1986. Recent trends also indicate no growth in the feminization of poverty. In 1981, 57.3 percent of all low-income Canadians were female; in 1986, that figure was 56.1 percent. For a more detailed discussion of women and poverty, see Gee and Kimball 1987, Chapter 4. This reference points out that while on the average the prevalence of poverty has declined for elderly women, because of the wide variance of poverty and wealth among the elderly, there are some segments of this population for which there has been no improvement.

TABLE 3.6

PERCENTAGE OF INCOME FROM EACH SOURCE, POOR AND NON-POOR
AGED COUPLES AND UNATTACHED INDIVIDUALS, 1981

Income Source	Aged Couples*		Aged Unattached Individuals	
	Poor	Non-Poor	Poor	Non-Poor
OAS/GIS	78.7%	31.6%	74.6%	19.6%
Other government	3.2	2.8	4.5	2.8
C/QPP	11.3	9.1	7.7	8.8
Total public	93.2	43.5	86.8	31.2
Private pensions	2.3	12.0	3.3	15.3
Investments	3.8	28.8	8.6	42.3
Employment	0.7	14.4	0.8	8.9
Total private	6.8	56.5	13.2	68.8
Total	100.0	100.0	100.0	100.0

*Couples in which both spouses were 65 or older in 1981.
SOURCE: National Council of Welfare 1984a, 44.

As expected, sources of income for the elderly poor are different from those of the non-poor (see Table 3.6).

The National Council of Welfare (1984a) stated that, in 1981, half of the elderly in Canada had so little retirement income that they qualified for at least a partial Guaranteed Income Supplement. The average senior citizen gets about half of his or her income from public sources (National Council of Welfare 1984b, 72).

For those existing solely on OAS, GIS, and provincial supplements, Table 3.7 shows the difference between their income and the Statistics Canada low-income line for 1989.

Thus, while we have made significant strides in providing economic security to the elderly, there are still many elderly Canadians not guaranteed a basic living income, the first requirement for economic security as defined in Chapter 1 (see also Chapters 4 and 5).

3.7 WEALTH AND INCOME — DISPARITY OF DISTRIBUTION

A poll taken in January 1985 reported that 84 percent of Canadians over 65 are satisfied with their personal economic circumstances, and 75 percent express optimism about their economic future. Only 14 percent said they wanted more money as their first priority, whereas 76 percent wanted better health (Brown, R.L. 1987, 10).

TABLE 3.7

DIFFERENCE BETWEEN MAXIMUM GOVERNMENT
BENEFITS FOR THE ELDERLY AND THE POVERTY LINE, 1989

	Single Persons		Couples	
	Maximum Income from Governments	Difference From Proverty Line	Maximum Income from Governments	Difference From Proverty Line
St. John's	$8,644	-$2,788	$14,014	-$1,060
Charlottetown	8,644	-2,081	14,014	-49
Halifax	8,863	-2,569	14,052	-622
St. John	8,644	-2,788	14,014	-1,060
Montreal	8,644	-3,393	14,014	-1,867
Toronto	9,640	-2,397	16,006	+125
Winnipeg	9,065	-2,972	14,920	-961
Saskatchewan	9,604	-1,828	15,634	+560
Edmonton	9,784	-2,253	16,294	+413
Vancouver	9,236	-2,801	15,460	-421
Whitehorse	9,844	-71	16,414	+3,366
Yellowknife	9,844	-71	16,414	+3,366

SOURCE: National Council of Welfare 1989b, 17.

As noted, savings rates do not peak until age 67 and remain positive at all advanced ages. In the Gallop poll (Allenvest Group Limited 1985) referred to in Chapter 1, 45 percent of the retirees reported that they are still able to add to their savings each year. Denton and Spencer (Task Force on Inflation Protection, Vol. 1 1988, 226) report that investment income as a source of income for the elderly continues to rise with age up to the 70-74 age group and, in the case of married couples, into the 80-and-over range.

The overall impression that arises from the literature is the disparity of wealth and income among the elderly in Canada. A calculation that is sometimes used to verify disparity of income is the ratio of average income for all members of the group versus the income of the median individual in the group. For families with a head of household aged 45 to 54, this ratio is 1.1. For families with an elderly head of household (65+), this ratio is 1.4 (Brown, R.L. 1982, 16). This indicates that income is not distributed symmetrically around the average or mean. Rather, this indicates a distribution in income that is skewed to the higher income levels. That is, statistics suggest that while there are many poor elderly, there are also many wealthy elderly. In fact, there are a sufficient number of wealthy elderly that marketing executives are viewing them as an important target market. "Seniors are not only swelling in number but also in consumer power. In marketing lingo, they are alternatively called Prime Timers, the New Old, the Vintage Generation, and Wellderly" (Aisenberg 1987).

Data from Statistics Canada (1986a) show that 66 percent of over-65 households own their own homes, and only seven percent have a mortgage. This, in combination with the fact that dependent children are no longer a cash drain, means that many elderly have relatively high amounts of discretionary income.

3.8 REPLACEMENT RATIOS

Chapter 1 noted two criteria for economic security. First, one must be assured of income that is above an accepted measure of poverty. Second, one expects to maintain a certain standard of living, that is, to provide a certain replacement ratio of pre-retirement income. Just what that replacement ratio should be is the subject of debate. However, one does not need to replace one's entire pre-retirement gross income to maintain one's standard of living. There are many reasons for this.

First, as noted previously, at age 65 many tax concessions take effect. Further, there is a significant decrease in many expenses at the time of retirement. For example, all work-related expenses end, as do deductions for pension contributions and health insurance plans (government or private supplementary). Mortgage payments also usually end.

The replacement ratio required for economic security (maintenance of one's standard of living and a basic floor of protection) will vary by the level of pre-retirement income. For the working poor, even a full 100 percent replacement ratio may not bring them above the poverty level. However, for the wealthy, a replacement ratio of 60 percent of pre-retirement income would probably allow full economic security (see also Section 6.2).

As noted earlier in this chapter, one should use a cohort analysis which looks at the replacement ratios of members of one generation rather than cross-sectional data which compare different age groups at one point in time. Such cohort data are shown in Table 3.8.

It should be noted that the effects of inflation have been taken into account by expressing values in constant 1984 dollars. Denton and Spencer draw two conclusions from these data:

> The main observation from this table is that while incomes do indeed decline with retirement, average incomes for 65-69-year-olds have fairly typically been 85 to 95 percent of what they were for (approximately) the same people five years before, when they were five years younger. However, this calculation probably understates somewhat the actual deterioration in income position over this age interval, since the percentage of males filing income tax returns is higher for 60-64-year-olds than for 65-69-year-olds and the percentage has been rising for the former and falling for the latter.

TABLE 3.8

AVERAGE TOTAL INCOME, BEFORE AND AFTER AGE 65, FOR ALL MALES FILING INCOME TAX RETURNS, 1963-84 (1984 DOLLARS)

Ages 60-64		Ages 65-69		Income at Ages 65-69 As % of Income at
Year	Income	Year	Income	Ages 60-64
1963	17,652	1968	15,569	88.2
1964	18,143	1969	16,071	88.6
1965	18,995	1970	16,194	85.3
1966	18,622	1971	16,162	86.8
1967	19,091	1972	17,131	89.7
1968	19,537	1973	17,869	91.5
1969	20,225	1974	19,075	94.3
1970	20,622	1975	19,413	94.1
1971	21,276	1976	19,636	92.3
1972	22,477	1977	19,784	88.0
1973	23,631	1978	20,034	84.8
1974	24,993	1979	20,826	83.3
1975	25,376	1980	22,471	88.6
1976	25,984	1981	22,649	87.2
1977	26,372	1982	22,212	84.2
1978	25,942	1983	21,297	82.1
1979	26,965	1984	22,236	82.5

SOURCE: Task Force on Inflation Protection 1988, Vol. 1, 235.

The general pattern of age-income change reported suggests at the very least, that the average income position of the elderly did not decline relative to other age groups even with the high inflation levels during much of the data period (Task Force on Inflation Protection 1988, Vol. 1, 224).

3.9 CONCLUSIONS

This monograph defines economic security as "a state of mind or sense of well-being whereby an individual is relatively certain that he or she can satisfy basic needs and wants, both present and future." Chapter 1 explained that this definition leads to two requirements; namely, that a basic income floor be achieved, and that one's standard of living not be significantly disrupted.

There are indications that many elderly Canadians experience economic insecurity because they live in poverty. At the same time, many elderly Canadians are wealthy and achieve high income replacement ratios in retirement and can be said to have achieved full economic security based on the two stated criteria.

According to a poll (Allenvest Group Limited 1985), 45 percent of those who were retired reported that they are still able to save. In fact, 67 percent of those with company pension plans are net savers. Sixty-three percent of retirees reported feeling economically secure, while 28 percent reported not feeling secure. Those with savings plans or a company pension plan had a higher probability of feeling economically secure (75 percent).

Non-income subsidies are an important source of economic security for the elderly. As pointed out by Nowak (1988, 181):

> In 1976 almost 20 percent of spending units (families or individuals) aged 65 and over reported rent subsidies. The federal government allows special tax exemptions for older people, like the age exemption on income tax above the personal exemption (Health and Welfare Canada 1982b). Also, corporations offer subsidies for goods and services, like reduced theatre ticket prices or reduced air fares for older people. Stone and McLean (1979) say that these indirect subsidies could add at least 30 percent to older people's average total income, and this does not count other benefits such as subsidized health care costs and home care services.

The next three chapters explore sources of retirement income security that exist in Canada: government-sponsored (Chapter 4), employer-sponsored (Chapter 5), and self-initiated (Chapter 6).

These plans are analysed to see where each one fits into the two requirements for financial security: a basic floor of income and a consistent standard of living. Each plan is also reviewed in terms of its relevance to today's economic realities for the elderly in Canada; which plans are well suited to solving the disparity of economic security that now prevails, and which ones are ill-suited. Finally, these chapters consider reform proposals in light of the fact that there are some elderly Canadians who can afford to shoulder more of the burden of providing financial security for all elderly Canadians.

APPENDIX

Provincial Income Supplementation Programs

		Maximum Annual Benefit 1989	
		Single Person	Two-Pensioner Couple
Nova Scotia:	Special Social Assistance	$219	$438
Ontario:	GAINS-A (Guaranteed Annual Income System)	996	1,992
Manitoba:	55 Plus — at Manitoba Income Supplement	421	906
Saskatchewan:	Saskatchewan Income Plan	960	1,620
Alberta:	Alberta Assured Income Plan Alberta Widows' Pension	1,140	2,280
British Columbia:	GAIN for Seniors Supplement (Guaranteed Available Income for Need)	592	1,446
Yukon:	Income Supplement Program for Seniors	1,200	2,400
NWT:	Senior Citizens Benefits	1,200	2,400

Provincial Taxation and Shelter Assistance Programs for Seniors

Newfoundland:	School Tax Exemption
Prince Edward Island:	Tax Deferral for Senior Citizens Residential Property Tax Credit
Nova Scotia:	Property Tax Rebate for Senior Citizens Rental Assistance Program
New Brunswick:	Assistance for the Reduction of Rental Costs
Quebec:	LOGIRENTE (Senior Citizens' Rental Assistance Program) Real Estate Tax Refund
Ontario:	Property Tax Grant Sales Tax Grant
Manitoba:	School Tax Assistance for Tenants 55 Plus Pensioner Homeowners' School Tax Assistance Property Tax Credit Shelter Allowances for Elderly Renters
Saskatchewan:	Senior Citizens' Heritage Program Saskatchewan Tax Reductions
Alberta:	Property Tax Reduction Benefits (including Senior Homeowner Refund) Senior Citizens' Renter Assistance Grant Senior Citizens' Home Heating Protection Program
British Columbia:	Land Tax Deferment Program Home Owner Grant Shelter Aid for Elderly Renters

Provincial Income Supplementation Programs, cont'd

Yukon:	Home Owners' Grant
	Pioneer Utility Grant
NWT:	Senior Citizens' Land Tax Relief

Source: Health and Welfare Canada 1989a, Preface; and National Council of Welfare 1989b, 14.

GOVERNMENT-SPONSORED INCOME SECURITY

4.1 INTRODUCTION

Canada's retirement income security system has recently undergone significant reform. In *Better Pensions for Canadians* (Canada 1982), the government identified three principles as the basis for improvements to the retirement income system; namely:

- elderly Canadians should be guaranteed a reasonable minimum level of income;
- the opportunities and arrangements available to Canadians should be fair; and
- Canadians should be able to avoid serious disruption of their pre-retirement living standards upon retirement.

These goals are consistent with our criteria for economic security as outlined in Chapters 1 and 3.

Chapter 4 will analyse the place of government-sponsored income security programs within a total system which has three tiers of support and sponsorship: the government (Chapter 4), the employer (Chapter 5), and the individual (Chapter 6). It will also show that the government-sponsored system leaves room for individual initiative and flexibility that, in turn, encourage the accumulation of funds that can be used to fuel the economy.

4.2 BACKGROUND AND HISTORY

When provincial and federal rights were divided at the time of Confederation in 1867, the provinces were given jurisdiction over matters relevant to health, education, and welfare. It was widely accepted that these provincial rights included the payment of pensions (Longhurst and Earle 1987, 6). This division of power kept the federal government out of the income security field for the first sixty years of Confederation.

In 1927, using the "grant-in-aid" provision, the federal government entered the pension area through the *Old Age Pensions Act,* R.S.C. 1927, c. 156 (a similar process was later used to enter the health field; see Section 7.2). The *Old Age Pensions Act* offered to pay 50 percent (later raised to 75 percent) of the cost of means-tested pensions to be paid and administered by the provinces. The maximum pension would be $20 a month to persons over age 70 who met certain citizenship and residence requirements and who could pass a needs test. Individuals were not required to contribute. By 1951, benefits had risen to $40 a month (the 1990 equivalent is $234 a month).

The *Old Age Pensions Act* was replaced by the *Old Age Security* (OAS) *Act* R.S.C. 1952, c. 200. OAS benefits of $40 a month would be paid at age 70 regardless of need. A means-tested pension, also $40 a month, would be available to those aged 65 to 69. This plan remained in force for the next fifteen years, although benefits were increased several times.

The next major reform came into effect on January 1, 1966, when the contributory, earnings-related Canada/Quebec Pension Plan (C/QPP), was introduced, although full retirement income benefits were not paid until 1976. The C/QPP promised retirement benefits equal to 25 percent of credited earnings (up to the Average Industrial Wage). Hence, the provision of economic security through government-sponsored systems was greatly expanded.

At that time several other changes were also put into effect. The universal Old Age Security (OAS) system qualification age (without need) was lowered from age 70 to age 65 over a five-year period. The Guaranteed Income Supplement (GIS) was added to OAS as a temporary measure to cover the ten-year transitional period of C/QPP implementation, providing income-tested benefits for those with no or low C/QPP benefits. However, this temporary add-on is still with us and has remained an essential element of the government income security system. At the same time, several provinces also introduced supplements (*e.g.,* Ontario GAINS) for their residents. These were all needs or income tested.

When the GIS was introduced it provided, in combination with the OAS pension, an income guarantee to single pensioners equal to about 25 percent of the average wage. A pensioner couple were guaranteed an income equal to about half the average wage.

In 1975, the Spouse's Allowance (SPA) was added. It is payable to OAS pensioners' spouses, of either sex, aged 60-64 on an income-tested level. These households are thus guaranteed a minimum income equivalent to that of a GIS pensioner couple.

Prior to the introduction of the OAS program in 1952, Canada's elderly had suffered relative economic hardship. In 1951, the median income of unattached individuals aged 65 and over, the majority of whom would be women, was 36.4 percent of the median income of all Canadians, and that for families headed by a person aged 65 and over was 51.4 percent of the median income of all families. By 1983, the same statistics were 74.9 percent and 60.1 percent, respectively (International Social Security Association 1984, 108). Most of this enhancement in economic security was due to the introduction of government-sponsored social security systems such as OAS, GIS, and C/QPP, as indicated by the data of Table 3.1.

4.3 OLD AGE SECURITY (OAS)

Everyone in Canada aged 65 or over who is a citizen or a legal resident may qualify for either a full or partial OAS pension. The pension normally begins in the month following the person's 65th birthday. The OAS pension is universal for those 65 years of age and over, subject only to residence requirements. No income or asset tests are applied.

There are two methods of meeting residency requirements for a *full pension*. Canadians 25 years of age or over on July 1, 1977, qualify with 10 years of residence immediately prior to application. Persons who were not yet 25 qualify for a full pension with 40 years of residence in Canada after age 18. Those not qualified for a full pension may receive a *partial pension*, on a pro-rated basis, provided they have at least 10 years' residence.

Reciprocal International Social Security Agreements exist with other countries. Thus, a person residing in Canada may add those periods of residence in a reciprocating country to his years of residence in Canada in order to qualify for the OAS pension. The OAS pension may be paid indefinitely outside of Canada if the pensioner has 20 years of residence in Canada after age 18. Otherwise, it may be paid for six months outside of Canada and resumed when the pensioner returns to Canada.

Persons meeting the residence requirements for OAS receive the full pension, which, as of January 1, 1990, was $340.07. This benefit is fully indexed to the cost of living as measured by the Consumer Price Index. Benefit increases take place quarterly. A partial OAS pension is calculated at the rate of 1/40th of the full pension for each year of residence in Canada for those who have at least 10 years' residence. OAS benefits are paid from general tax revenues and are taxable income. In 1986/87, OAS was paid to 2.7 million Canadians with payments totalling $9.5 billion (Health and Welfare Canada 1989a, 17, 19).

While OAS has been indexed to the cost of living since 1971, its importance in the total income security package has slipped over the last 25 years. In 1964, OAS benefits represented a level equal to 20 percent of the Average Industrial Wage. By 1983, that level had declined to 14 percent (Treasurer of Ontario 1984, 28). The importance of OAS will continue to decline without explicit amendments since wages normally rise faster than the cost of living, due to productivity gains. Thus, OAS will no longer be the cornerstone of the government-sponsored income security system. The foundation will now be a combination of GIS and C/QPP benefits.

In 1985, the federal government debated the merits of the continued universality of OAS benefits (*i.e.*, no needs or income test). In addition, in its 1985 budget, the government proposed to partially de-index the OAS, adjusting only for cost-of-living increases in excess of 3 percent per annum. This provision was abandoned in the face of strong opposition from senior citizens' groups.

However, in its 1989 budget, the federal government introduced measures that will tax-back the OAS benefit from recipients with net income in excess of $50,000 a year.[1] As pointed out by the National Council of Welfare (1989a, 1): "this marks the end of universality, a fundamental and long-standing principle of Canada's system of social benefits." The $50,000 limit is not indexed but will be adjusted occasionally by the government. To the extent that these ad hoc adjustments fall behind inflation, more and more Canadians will face the tax-back. This tax-back of benefits from the wealthy changes OAS from a "demogrant" benefit (*i.e.*, payable to all, based on a residence test only) to a second-tier of the Guaranteed Income Supplement (GIS).

4.4 GUARANTEED INCOME SUPPLEMENT (GIS)

OAS pensioners with little or no income may receive full or partial GIS benefits. Only the GIS portion of the total OAS/GIS benefit is subject to reduction because of other income. If a pensioner leaves Canada, the Supplement is paid for six months and is then discontinued until his/her return.

The amount of GIS to which an individual is entitled is determined by marital status and income. If the pensioner is married, the combined income of the pensioner and spouse is taken into account. The value of any assets which the household may have does not affect eligibility for GIS. Income for GIS purposes is, for the most part, net taxable income except OAS benefits, federal Family Allowances, and the Child Tax Credit.

There are two rates for the GIS. One applies to single pensioners (including widowed, divorced, or separated persons) and also to married pensioners whose spouses are not in receipt of either the OAS pension or the Spouse's Allowance. The other applies to spouses in married couples where both spouses are pensioners.

For a single pensioner, the maximum monthly Supplement is reduced by $1 for each $2 of income. For a married couple where both spouses are in receipt of the basic OAS pension, the maximum monthly Supplement of *each* pensioner is reduced by $1 for every $4 of their *combined* monthly income.

A special provision applies for a married couple in which only one spouse is a pensioner and the other is not eligible for either the basic OAS pension or the Spouse's Allowance, whereby the pensioner is entitled to receive the GIS at the higher rate paid to single persons; moreover, the maximum monthly Supplement is reduced by only $1 for every $4 of the couple's combined monthly income (excluding the OAS benefit). Benefits are indexed quarterly according to the Consumer Price Index. GIS payments are made out of general tax revenues; no contributions are required.

The maximum monthly benefit as at January 1, 1990, was $404.13 (single) and $263.23 each (married). Additional supplements of varying amounts are also paid by six provinces and two territories (see Chapter 3, Appendix). For example, the Ontario GAINS automatically paid up to $83 a month extra as at January 1, 1989, for anyone receiving GIS. GAINS is also reduced by $1 for every $2 of additional income. The result of this reduction (50 percent) added to the GIS reduction means that at the transitional level, for every $2 of income earned, the total GIS/GAINS payment is reduced $2. GIS benefits are non-taxable, although those eligible for GIS would probably not pay tax regardless. In 1986-87, there were 1.3 million GIS beneficiaries, and benefit payments totalled $3.5 billion (Health and Welfare Canada 1989a, 17, 19).

GIS benefit levels have been increased several times since its inception (over and above the automatic cost-of-living increases), and it is now a significant part of the retirement income security system in Canada.

4.5 SPOUSE'S ALLOWANCE (SPA)

The spouse of an OAS pensioner may be eligible for a Spouse's Allowance (SPA) if the spouse is 60 to 64 years of age and has 10 years' residence in Canada. Once the residence requirements have been met, eligibility is subject to an income test similar to that for GIS. The benefit ceases to be payable if the couple becomes separated or divorced, or if the SPA recipient dies.

The spouse who is eligible for an SPA when the OAS pensioner spouse dies retains eligibility for the SPA until age 65, or until remarriage. This provision, known as Extended SPA, was implemented in 1979. A 1985 amendment provides for payment of a Spouse's Allowance to any widow(er) who is between the ages of 60 and 64 who has been a Canadian resident for at least ten years prior to the date of application.

For couples, the SPA benefit is based on their combined annual income, whereas for beneficiaries of Extended SPA and Widowed SPA, it is based on the surviving spouse's income only. Assets are not considered for entitlement.

The maximum full monthly SPA is equal to the full basic OAS pension plus maximum GIS at the married rate. The SPA is reduced by $3 for every $4 of the couple's combined monthly income until the OAS equivalent is eliminated. After that, the GIS equivalent of the SPA and the GIS of the pensioner are each reduced by $1 for every additional $4 of combined monthly income.

For the Extended Spouse's Allowance (and Widowed SPA effective September 1985), the maximum monthly allowance is reduced by $3 for every $4 of the surviving spouse's monthly income until the OAS equivalent is eliminated; it is then reduced by $1 for every additional $2 of monthly income.

SPA benefit payments are made from general tax revenues (*i.e.*, no contributions are required). As at January 1, 1990, the maximum monthly allowance to spouses was $603.30, and to widows and widowers was $666.05. Benefits are indexed quarterly to match the cost of living. In 1986-87 the number of SPA beneficiaries was 143,764, and the total payment made was $473 million (Health and Welfare Canada 1989a, 17, 19). For those who qualify, the SPA has the effect of providing the same guaranteed income to the pensioner's family as would be provided by OAS plus GIS, if both husband and wife were pensioners.

The combination of the OAS/GIS/SPA programs is thus designed to provide a minimum floor of security. The minimum income guarantee for single, widowed, and divorced pensioners is about one-third of the Average Industrial Wage, while that for pensioner couples is approximately one-half of the Average Industrial Wage (International Social Security Association 1986, 9).

While these plans provide a minimum floor of security, they do little to satisfy the requirement of maintaining a consistent standard of living. The only government-sponsored program that does so is the Canada/Quebec Pension Plan.

4.6 CANADA AND QUEBEC PENSION PLAN (C/QPP)

The Canada Pension Plan and Quebec Pension Plan (Régime de rentes du Quebec) were introduced in 1966, and are compulsory contributory social insurance plans. The Canada Pension Plan (CPP) operates in all regions of Canada, except Quebec. Both plans provide retirement, disability, and survivors' pensions, disabled contributors' children's benefits, orphans' benefits, and death benefits. The plans are reciprocal, to ensure coverage for all adult Canadians in the labour force.

The plans are similar in terms of eligibility criteria, benefits, and financing. The following description applies to both plans (differences are noted where relevant):

Eligibility

The C/QPP is financed by compulsory contributions between ages 18 and 65, based on earned income. Persons over 65 who are still in the labour force have the option of contributing until age 70. Persons already receiving disability or retirement benefits or those with earnings below a certain minimum, which is known as the Year's Basic Exemption ($2,800 in 1990), do not contribute. All benefits under C/QPP are payable regardless of where the beneficiary lives, whether in Canada or abroad.

Spouses working in small unincorporated businesses such as family farms, fishing operations, and neighborhood stores are also eligible to contribute to the C/QPP. It is estimated that as many as half a million couples own and operate small unincorporated businesses in Canada. This greatly increases the number of women able to qualify for C/QPP benefits.

Pension credits earned by one or both spouses during marriage will be divided equally in the event of divorce or legal annulment. This division is mandatory. In the case of separation either spouse may apply for a division of pension credits after one year has elapsed.

Reciprocal International Social Security Agreements exist with certain other countries to avoid duplication of coverage, to ensure that no one is left without coverage, and to ensure that eligible persons may contribute under the plan of one country or the other. To establish eligibility for C/QPP benefits, persons residing in Canada may add the credits which they have earned under the social security system of a reciprocating country to their Canadian credits.

Eligibility for C/QPP benefits is not based on income or assets but on contributions. Retirement, survivor's, disability, and death benefit levels are based on the average adjusted pensionable career earnings of the contributor (see "Benefits," below). The orphan's and disabled contributor's child's benefit amounts are not related to these career earnings.

Benefits

The C/QPP provide the following monthly benefits which are treated as taxable income: a retirement pension, a disability pension, a surviving spouse's pension, a disabled contributor's child's benefit, and an orphan's benefit. Once benefits are in place, they are adjusted annually to the Consumer Price Index.

Contributory Period

The C/QPP contributory period starts at the latter part of January 1966 or age 18 and ends when the beneficiary ceases earning or turns 70. There are provisions which allow a person to drop, from the contributory period, months of low or zero earnings totalling up to 15 percent of the total period. This drop-out provision, however, cannot reduce the contributory period to less than 10 years. Should an individual choose to defer application for a retirement pension beyond age 65, months of pensionable earnings after age 65 may be substituted for months of low or no pensionable earnings prior to age 65. Any month during which a disability pension was paid is excluded from the contributory period.

A special child-rearing drop-out provision allows for the exclusion of any months of low or zero earnings which occurred when a person was caring for a child under age seven and was in receipt of Family Allowance benefits in respect of the child.

Retirement Pension

A retirement pension is payable to a person who is aged 60 or over who has made one valid contribution to CPP or for at least one year to QPP. Persons aged 60-64 who apply for this pension must have retired from work; C/QPP applicants over 65 are eligible for a retirement pension regardless of whether or not they have stopped working. Once a retirement pension becomes payable, or a person reaches age 70, no further C/QPP contributions can be made.

The annual retirement pension is equal to 25 percent of average adjusted pensionable career earnings received during the contributory period. Pensionable career earnings are earnings for each eligible year worked up to the Year's Maximum Pensionable Earnings (YMPE), which is approximately equal to the Average Industrial Wage. Roughly speaking, one's historic earnings are adjusted upward in line with the Average Industrial Wage. The maximum retirement pension is then calculated to be 25 percent of one's career average earnings so adjusted.

Payment of the retirement pension can begin between the ages of 60 and 70. The "regular" pension is payable at age 65. For persons retiring between ages 60 and 64, this pension is reduced by 0.5 percent for each month left until their 65th birthday (or 6 percent per year). Persons under age 65 who apply must have wholly or substantially ceased working. Persons who delay retirement beyond 65 have their pension increased by 0.5 percent for each month of delay from their 65th birthday until they receive their first pension payment (up to their 70th birthday). The maximum change in the pension is thus 30 percent. Once the entitlement is calculated, the pension remains the same except for annual indexation to the cost of living.

Surviving Spouse's Pension

Benefits are payable to the surviving spouse of a deceased contributor, providing contributions have been made for a minimum qualifying period. Payment to a common-law spouse is subject to further legislated conditions.

A benefit consisting of a defined dollar portion and 37.5 percent of the contributor's retirement pension is payable to a surviving spouse aged 45 to 64 years, or to a surviving spouse under age 45 who is disabled or has dependent children. There is a pro-rated reduction in this benefit when the surviving spouse is between the ages 35 and 45, is not disabled, and has no dependent children. A spouse who is under age 35 when widowed, and is neither disabled nor has dependent children, is not eligible for a surviving spouse's pension before reaching age 65, unless he/she subsequently becomes disabled.

A surviving spouse over age 65 receives a benefit equal to 60 percent of the contributor's retirement pension at the time of the contributor's death. Remarriage used to, but no longer, means a loss of this benefit.

Financing

The C/QPP are funded through employer and employee contributions plus interest earned on surplus funds. The CPP excess funds are lent to the provinces in proportion to the province's contributions to the Plan. The Quebec Deposit and Investment Fund (Caisse de dépôt et de placement du Quebec) manages the excess QPP funds.

Employee contributions to CPP or QPP in 1990 were made at a rate of 2.2 percent of contributory earnings, these being earnings falling between the Year's Basic Exemption (YBE) of $2,800 and the Year's Maximum Pensionable Earnings (YMPE) of $28,900 in 1990. Persons earning incomes at or above the YMPE pay the maximum contribution. Employers match the employee's contributions, while self-employed persons contribute the total 4.4 percent themselves. The contribution rate will rise gradually to 7.6 percent (3.8 + 3.8) in 2011 because of plan maturation and population aging, and further increases are anticipated (see Section 8.2).

As of January 1, 1990, the maximum monthly retirement benefit was $403.96 at age 60, $577.08 at age 65, and $750.20 at age 70. This is taxable income to the recipient. In 1986-87, 1.8 million Canadians received C/QPP retirement benefits totalling $5.1 billion. A further 618,000 persons received $1.4 billion in surviving spouse's pensions (Health and Welfare Canada 1989a, 144-46). Since the C/QPP has only existed since 1966 and only paid full benefits to those retiring since 1976, the above benefit amounts can be expected to rise rapidly (Canada, Office of the Superintendent of Financial Institutions 1988).

There are many advantages to the C/QPP. Coverage is universal and automatic for those employed and earning at least 10 percent of the Average Industrial Wage. In 1981, 91 percent of men and 63 percent of women aged 20 to 64 contributed to the C/QPP (National Council of Welfare 1984b, 37). Benefits are immediately fully **vested** and fully **portable** (these terms are explained in Section 5.5). They are indexed before retirement to the Average Industrial Wage and after retirement to the cost of living.

However, coverage does not extend to the never employed, the chronically unemployed, or the very poor since a person must have earned income at least equal to 10 percent of the Average Industrial Wage to earn benefit credits. Consequently, homemakers are the largest group of Canadians not covered. While the government continues to promise coverage to homemakers, no legislation has been proposed to date. For these Canadians, economic security in retirement is reduced, since the maximum C/QPP benefits available to them is the 60 percent survivor's benefit upon the death of the income-earning spouse.

Increasing benefit levels under C/QPP would do almost nothing for the very poor, the chronically unemployed, or never employed (*e.g.*, homemakers). For those now eligible for GIS, increases in C/QPP benefits will mean decreased GIS benefits. For example, consider a couple in Ontario eligible for both GIS and GAINS. In 1983, the addition of a maximum CPP pension of $4,141 to the income of this elderly couple would have increased their overall annual income by only $162 (Ontario Economic Council 1983, 52). However, while GIS is funded from general tax reserves, the C/QPP is funded by contributions on earnings, so the end result would be regressive; that is, the low income worker would pay the increased costs of contributions for little in extra benefits.

Chapter 8 will analyse another issue surrounding the C/QPP; namely, its future funding.

4.7 REPLACEMENT RATIOS AND POVERTY

In Section 3.6, the significant decrease in poverty because of the government-sponsored income security system was discussed. Figure 4.1 shows the income replacement in retirement provided by government programs for a one-earner couple in 1984.

Low wage earners actually increase their net after-tax income after retirement, while those at the upper income levels are expected to provide more of their retirement income through employer-sponsored or personal savings plans (for which tax concessions are available). It would appear that the C/QPP was consciously limited to allow for this flexibility and to encourage the growth of investment funds that arise from private sector plans.

A 1984 report (National Council of Welfare 1984a, 42) states that government-sponsored schemes accounted for 45.5 percent of the total incomes of elderly couples, made up of 33.5 percent for OAS/GIS; 9.2 percent for C/QPP; and the balance from a variety of government sources, both federal and provincial. For unattached individuals, governments provided 51.3 percent of total incomes (39.6 percent from OAS/GIS and 8.4 percent from C/QPP).

Low income senior citizens get virtually all their income from government sources. The importance of government-sponsored income also rises with age (see Table 3.3, or Denton *et al.*, 1984b, 73) so that, as Canadians age, their income levels become more nearly alike.

The individual with the least economic security appears to be the unattached individual with no CPP benefits, most often an elderly woman (see

FIGURE **4.1**

INCOME REPLACEMENT IN RETIREMENT PROVIDED BY GOVERNMENT
PROGRAMS FOR ONE-EARNER COUPLE IN 1984

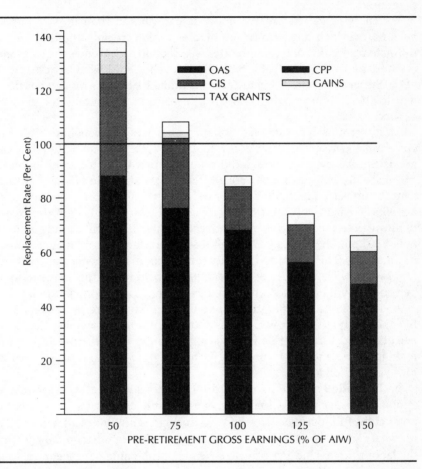

SOURCE: Treasurer of Ontario 1984, 22.

also Section 3.6). Presumably with the increased participation of women in the C/QPP and with pension reform (especially with respect to survivors' benefits) this, too, will change (see Section 5.5).

4.8 PUBLIC POLICY ISSUES

Funding Mode

Canadian government income security schemes are funded on a "pay-as-you-go" system (as are almost all government-sponsored schemes world-wide) whereby monies paid in today as contributions by one individual are immediately paid out as benefits to another individual. For OAS and GIS/SPA, there are no contributions, as benefits are paid from general tax revenues.

For the C/QPP, at present, more is contributed than is paid out in benefits, even at today's contribution rates, which are only one-third of the ultimate projected contribution rates (see Section 8.2). Hence, the CPP had accumulated a "surplus" of $38.8 billion by year-end, 1988 (Canada, Office of the Superintendent of Financial Institutions 1988). This money has been lent to the provinces which, in turn, have used the money for general expenditures.

Many groups have lobbied for increased C/QPP benefits. With the current 4.4 percent contribution rate, the C/QPP is financially advantageous. Similar benefits provided through the private sector would require a contribution rate of about 9 percent (Treasurer of Ontario 1984, 38). In fact, contributions to date have paid for only about one-third of the promised benefits (Treasurer of Ontario 1984, 37). As at December 31, 1988, the excess of future promised benefits over the accumulated $38.8 billion surplus was over $300 billion (Canada, Office of the Superintendent of Financial Institutions 1988). This unfunded liability represents an intergenerational transfer of wealth. That is, the cost of benefits not paid for by this generation of pensioners will be passed on to the next generation of contributors.

As long as future generations are willing to pay future promised benefits, there is no problem with pay-as-you-go funding. However, the number of retired beneficiaries will rise significantly over the next 40 years, making the payment of future benefits more expensive for future contributors (see Section 8.2).

Fully-funded schemes (required by law for almost all private plans) stipulate that each individual must have accumulated assets large enough to cover the full cost of pension benefits during the lifetime of all retired plan members and the cost of future expected benefits for plan members now in the labour force. Under a private scheme, participants have a **contractual** agreement that their benefits will be paid. Such plans, therefore, are not affected by shifting demographics. They can be affected only by investment failure or bankruptcy of the funding sponsor.

Under the government schemes, participants have a **statutory** promise that their benefits will be paid. That is, contributors who are paying the benefits of their parents' generation rely on the promise that the next generation of Canadians will do likewise (see Chapter 8). The recent claw-back of OAS benefits illustrates the insecurity inherent in this statutory contract. If the voters so choose, benefits can be reduced or removed at any time.

Effect on National Savings

Because government-sponsored income security schemes are "funded" on a "pay-as-you-go" basis, no investable assets arise (the exception being the small QPP surplus which is invested in real assets). The question then arises whether these pay-as-you-go government schemes depress gross national savings. Although much has been written on this matter (*e.g.*, see Redja 1988, 137-39, and Perron 1987), the authors do not agree on the answer. That is, it is not as yet clear whether pay-as-you-go government sponsored systems assist or depress national savings.

Indexation of Pension Benefits

At present, all government-sponsored schemes are indexed to the cost of living as measured by the Consumer Price Index (CPI). Two issues arise. First, by indexing retirement income to the CPI, the continued purchasing power of seniors (to the extent that it comes from a government source) is guaranteed. However, seniors do not benefit from the enhanced productivity of active workers and, hence, their standard of living will fall relative to active workers, assuming that average wages rise faster than the cost of living (this is generally true, except during the early 1980s). To guarantee seniors a constant share of gross national product would require retirement benefits indexed to the Average Industrial Wage (AIW). Indexation to the CPI only guarantees constant purchasing power.

Second, if one accepts that indexation should be to prices and not wages, the question remains as to whether the CPI is the correct index to reflect the costs incurred by seniors. Again, much has been written on this topic. A recent and extensive study found that cost indices conformed closely with the CPI. In making its recommendation, the report states: "Our conclusion is therefore that the all-Canada CPI would likely be a satisfactory indexing standard for Ontario pensions if a price indexing formula were to be adopted" (Task Force on Inflation Protection 1988, Vol. 1, 290).

Flexible Retirement

Until 1987 for the CPP, and 1984 for the QPP, retirement benefits became payable no earlier than age 65. While this is still true for OAS benefits, C/QPP benefits can now be taken at a flexible retirement age, with an actuarial adjustment in benefit level (as mentioned earlier).

There has been some debate as to the level of adjustment in the benefit payable (1/2 percent per month). Analysis by the C/QPP actuary (see Canada, Office of the Superintendent of Financial Institutions 1988), has shown that the adjustment of 1/2 percent per month in benefit levels is justified, given today's mortality rates and certain economic assumptions (see Section 6.2).

A second issue is the effect the new flexible retirement benefits will have on the labour force participation rates of Canadians over the age of 60. In the past two decades, male labour force participation rates beyond age 60 have declined significantly. Although this is not the case for women, where participation rates beyond age 60 remained relatively level, their rates can be viewed as being in relative decline, since all other female age-specific participation rates have risen.

In Quebec, where QPP flexible retirement benefits have been available from age 60 to age 70 since 1984, 80 percent of retirees chose early retirement (prior to age 65) in the first half of 1984. It is impossible to know how much of this was caused by the shift to the flexible retirement benefits scheme within the QPP and how much was because of outside pressures for early retirement.

Benefits and Poverty

Given the advantages of the C/QPP system already cited, many Canadians have suggested an expansion of the C/QPP. As noted earlier, expansion would do nothing for workers who do not qualify for C/QPP benefits. For workers earning low incomes, but qualifying for C/QPP benefits, it would result in increased C/QPP contributions but little increase in total government-sponsored benefits because GIS/SPA benefits would be reduced $1 for every $2 of extra C/QPP income. For someone also receiving a provincial supplement such as the Ontario GAINS, the loss of GIS/GAINS would be dollar for dollar.

An important public policy question is whether these implicit marginal "tax" rates of 50 percent and 100 percent are "equitable." Also, such high rates discourage the marginal worker from seeking further income.

The largest identifiable group of seniors living in poverty are elderly unattached women; nearly 79 percent of all single GIS recipients are women (National Council of Welfare 1989b, 9). The following example illustrates one reason for this situation:

> Take the case of an elderly couple in which the man received an average new CPP retirement pension in October 1983. The couple received $521 in Old Age Security benefits, $286 from the Guaranteed Income Supplement and $234 from the husband's CPP retirement pension — for a total monthly retirement income of $1,041, which is just $52 above the poverty line for a metropolitan area. The widow got $261 from OAS, $191 from a GIS and a CPP survivor's benefit of $141, for a total monthly income of $593 — 25 percent below the poverty line. She must get by on 57 percent of the income coming into the household before her husband died, while it is generally accepted that a replacement ratio of 60 to 70 percent is necessary (National Council of Welfare 1984b, 38).

Again, there seems reason to debate the level of the CPP survivor's benefit (60 percent of the worker's pension). However, this matter will decrease in importance as more women earn CPP pensions in their own right as opposed to survivors' pensions as dependents.

Another solution would be to allow homemakers to participate in the C/QPP and earn retirement benefits. A poll showed that 77 percent favoured inclusion of homemakers in the C/QPP; fewer than one in five Canadians were opposed (Marshall 1987, 8). While the past two federal governments have admitted that the provision of a homemakers' pension under the C/QPP is an important issue, no acceptable method of participation has yet been formulated (see Brown 1981, 17; and National Council of Welfare 1989b, 32).

Universality of OAS Benefits

GIS/SPA benefits are paid based on an income test. C/QPP benefits are based on contributions which are tied to earned income. OAS benefits, however, are paid on a demogrant basis; that is, they are payable to anyone aged 65 or over who passes a residency test—nothing more. In 1984-85, $8.2 billion of OAS benefits were paid out. While this income is taxable, it has been estimated that only 17 percent of this money was returned to Ottawa in the form of tax revenue (National Council of Welfare 1989b, 4) under prior rules.

The move in May 1985, to de-index OAS benefits was the first outward sign that the "universality" of OAS payments was being questioned; that is, whether wealthy Canadians should receive a full OAS benefit. The cost of such payments was significant.

An article in the November 26, 1984 *Globe and Mail* quotes Revenue Canada statistics that show that 5,800 people who earned a before-tax income in excess of $250,000 a year in 1981 cashed over $5 million in old age pension benefits. Figures from Statistics Canada, quoted in the March 28, 1984, *Toronto Star*, show that in 1981 almost $600 million in OAS payments went to families with incomes greater than $30,000 a year. But, at least for now, universality is a sacred cow, and questioning universality is political suicide (Longhurst and Earle 1987, 12).

As stated previously, the federal government, in its April 1989 budget, legislated a tax-back scheme on OAS benefits paid to those whose net income exceeded $50,000 a year. While universality appears to be maintained, since everyone who qualifies receives an OAS cheque, in reality universality has ended. While this will result in significant cost savings, it changes the OAS system from a universal benefit to a second-tier GIS benefit. This represents a significant reduction of the benefits many Canadians were counting on during retirement.

Information to Canadians

One of the directions that reform of private pension plans has taken is to provide more information to participants (see Section 5.5). In answer to the limited information that Canadians have about their position concerning retirement income security, Health and Welfare Canada has launched a campaign to ensure that Canadians are informed about their contributions to, and benefits earned from, the CPP. All participants now receive on a regular basis (every three or four years) a personalized statement showing eligible earnings and death and disability benefits earned to date. Statements can be obtained once a year, on request. This information will greatly enhance the ability of individuals to plan for their future economic security requirements.

4.9 CONCLUSIONS

This chapter reviewed the major provisions of the government-sponsored income security systems. It noted that these are available not on a **contractual** basis (as are private plans) but on a **statutory** basis. By paying for the benefits of the present generation of retirees, today's workers are establishing a social contract in the expectation that the next generation of workers will likewise provide their retirement income benefits. As seen in the 1989 amendment to the OAS benefits, however, such contracts are easily amended so long as voters are supportive.

In the poll previously referred to (Allenvest Group Limited 1985), Canadians were asked if they would rather contribute to a government-sponsored retirement income scheme or some personal retirement scheme. Only 31 percent favoured the government-sponsored plan. However, when asked if they would rather contribute to a government-sponsored plan or have more cash income, 59 percent preferred the government plan, with 34 percent favouring increased income. Hence, we see no opposition to deferral of income *per se*, only a preference for personal plans.

When those surveyed were asked if they were worried about receiving their benefits, 36 percent said yes for GIS; 44 percent worried about OAS; and 42 percent showed concern over C/QPP benefits. Hence we sense levels of insecurity that indicate a need for heightened communication as to the security of these benefits.

The publicly administered retirement income systems are not intended to provide all the income needed in retirement. Indeed, when the C/QPP was introduced, it was designed deliberately to leave room for private retirement income schemes (International Social Security Association 1987, 106).

It is up to each Canadian to decide what level of retirement income security is desired and then set out a savings plan that will achieve that personal goal. However, there is a choice to be made, and it should be made with forethought.

In that regard, chapters 5 and 6 will describe the other two tiers of the retirement income support system.

NOTE

1 The amount of repayment required is equal to 15 percent of the taxpayer's income in excess of the $50,000 threshold, up to the total of the Federal Family allowances and OAS benefits included in the taxpayer's income.

CHAPTER 5

EMPLOYER-SPONSORED PENSION PLANS

5.1 INTRODUCTION

Chapter 4 showed that the government-sponsored OAS and GIS provide a basic floor of protection to all Canadians. It noted that the second criterion of economic security, namely to avoid a drastic change in standard of living on retirement, is **partly** satisfied by the C/QPP, although not for everyone. Any additional perceived or actual needs must be met through private sector sources. This chapter will analyse employer-sponsored pension plans, and Chapter 6, individual retirement savings plans.

Private provisions for improving one's replacement ratio have two advantages. First, the system is flexible. Target replacement ratios, calculated by Bassett varied from a high of 86 percent for the working poor to 51 percent for the more wealthy (Schulz 1985, 74). This wide divergence can best be satisfied through schemes tailored to the individual. The second advantage of the private system is that such plans represent an important source of investment dollars which can fund risk ventures upon which the Canadian economy depends. In general (the Quebec Pension Plan being an exception), government-sponsored schemes do not provide investable funds.

5.2 HISTORY AND BACKGROUND

In describing the genesis of private pension plans, Morton and McCallum state:

> Once again, pension plans were created to further a company's corporate goals of inspiring loyalty and cooperation among employees, raising morale and efficiency, cutting labour turnover, and inducing the retirement of older workers. In general, the introduction of pension plans helped to reduce labour strife. In 1919, the worst year for strikes in Canadian history, one corporate official explained that a pension plan "is not philanthropy and it is not benevolence: it is a cold-blooded business proposition," (Task Force on Inflation Protection, Vol. 1 1988, 12).

Despite these beginnings as pure business enticements, pensions grew rapidly in importance as one key aspect of employee benefit programs, especially after World War II, when unions took a more active interest in this employee benefit.

In the 1960s the government decided to regulate employment pension plans. Ontario was first, with its *Pension Benefits Act*, which came into effect January 1, 1965. This was followed by similar (but not identical) legislation in other jurisdictions. The fact that the provincial pension benefits Acts are not identical increases pension plan administration costs. To date, British Columbia and Prince Edward Island have not passed pension legislation.

These Acts had several objectives. Their primary concern was that the plans were adequately funded and that the funds were invested prudently (Ontario now has a Pension Guarantee Fund to further protect the benefits of workers whose pension plan might end). There were specific rules as to when employees gained rights to employer contributions (called **vesting**). Also, the Acts allowed the transferability of pension rights or assets when a worker changed jobs (called **portability**). Most of these Acts have undergone significant revisions, as noted later in this chapter.

5.3 EXISTING PLANS AND COVERAGE

Coverage:

Table 5.1 shows a breakdown of coverage of Canadian workers under employer-sponsored pension plans. The heading "Public Sector" means that the employer is the government; these are still private pension plans.

The data presented show the percentage C/QPP contributors (*i.e.*, most full-time workers) who are covered by private pension plans. Some cells show high levels of coverage, while others are much lower. In general, younger workers and women show lower levels of coverage. Also, the level of public sector coverage exceeds that in the private sector. The Report, *Ontario Proposals for Pension Reform*, provides an explanation of these differences in levels of coverage.

> This principally reflects the large number of small employers in the private sector who cannot generally afford to establish pension plans. In 1978, 2.7 million employees worked for 490,000 small businesses, with an average workforce of less than six individuals. Since only about one percent of all employees in the private sector were covered by plans with a membership of nine or less, the large number of small employers is a major reason for the lower level of private sector pension coverage.
>
> Because small employers often do not have employment pension plans, it should not be automatically concluded that supplementary provisions for retirement are not being made. Employees and employers can still contribute to individual or group RRSPs and accumulate real and financial assets. Data compiled by the Canadian Federation of Independent Business suggest that these latter vehicles are extensively used. When RRSPs and accumulation of real and financial assets are integrated into the definition of coverage, 90

percent of owners/managers and 83 percent of employees in the small businesses indicated they are making provisions for retirement (Treasurer of Ontario 1984, 21).

In September 1983, the Business Committee on Pension Policy (BCPP) reported that the persons not covered were primarily low income workers; employees under the age of 25; part-time workers; and employees of small employers. There are often acceptable reasons for this lack of coverage.

For many of these workers, membership in employment plans may not be desirable or necessary. For example, for persons under the age of 26 saving for retirement is not a high priority. Small employers may be financially unable to undertake the cost of a pension plan. In many cases, the small employer will provide other forms of savings such as a deferred profit sharing plan or ownership in the company (Longhurst and Earle 1987, 75).

Table 5.1

Percentage of C/QPP Contributors
Covered by Employer-Sponsored Pension Plans
By Income Levels, Age, and Sex, 1981+

Employment Income Range* $	Private Sector			Public Sector			Total Public/ Private
	Males %	Females %	Total %	Males %	Females %	Total %	%
1-9249	9.2	7.0	7.9	17.9	24.3	23.7	9.3
9250-18499	35.4	38.5	36.9	78.1	85.2	83.5	43.6
18500-27749	63.1	76.2	65.5	95.9	96.6	96.1	72.8
27750-36999	83.6	85.2	83.7	98.1	99.9	98.5	89.0
37000 or over	84.5	67.1	83.9	97.0	99.8	97.2	88.0
AGE GROUP							
18-24	15.8	11.8	14.0	51.9	53.7	52.8	18.5
25-44	51.0	32.7	43.3	90.5	79.5	85.8	51.9
45-54	68.3	34.0	54.7	92.3	82.6	89.0	61.5
55-64	78.3	45.5	65.8	91.1	80.6	87.9	70.5
65-70	58.4	28.8	45.3	72.0	55.5	62.6	50.1
TOTAL	47.4	28.1	39.3	86.0	74.9	81.4	47.0

*Income ranges are in increments of approximately half the average wage of the year in question (the average wage in 1981 = $18500)
+These figures do not include RRSP contributions

SOURCE: Health and Welfare Canada 1984, Table 1.

Most members of private pension plans belong to larger plans. In 1984, almost 85 percent of all plan members belonged to plans with more than 500 members, or fewer than 5 percent of the total number of existing plans (Task Force on Inflation Protection 1988, Report, 22).

Table 5.1 also shows that male participation rates in pension plans is generally higher than for females. One reason for this is the higher participation rates of female workers in industries where pension plan coverage is lower (*e.g.*, personal service industries) versus mining, construction, and manufacturing. Women also hold more part-time jobs which, until pension reform, did not earn pension credits.

Types of Plans

Pension plan statistics can be subdivided by plan type. One definition used for classification is based on whether the plan requires employee contributions (contributory plans) or not (non-contributory plans). According to Statistics Canada, in 1984 58 percent of the 17,711 pension plans in Canada were contributory, covering 69 percent of all plan members. Ninety-five percent of public sector plans were contributory, whereas only 57 percent of private plans required employee contributions (Task Force on Inflation Protection 1988, Report, 31).

Pension plans are also classed according to the method used to determine the contributions and benefits. There are two broad categories. In a **defined benefit plan**, the amount of the member's retirement benefit is specified in advance. The benefit can be a function of earnings and years of service or may be defined as a fixed dollar amount for each month or year of service (flat benefit). This benefit is promised by the plan sponsor who then builds up a fund to fulfil the promise. The risk that the pension funding variables (*e.g.*, rate of investment income earned) may deviate from the expected amount is borne by the plan sponsor, normally the employer.

TABLE 5.2

PENSION TYPES, AND PARTICIPANTS, 1982

Pension type	Plans		Active Members (000)	
	#	%	#	%
Defined Contribution	6,108	(40.1)	246	(5.3)
Defined Benefit				
flat benefit	1,340	(8.8)	1,039	(22.3)
% of earnings	7,345	(48.8)	3,324	(71.4)
Other	349	(2.3)	49	(1.0)

SOURCE: Statistics Canada 1984a, *Pension Plans in Canada*, 1982, 27.

In a **defined contribution plan**, frequently called a money purchase plan, the pension contract specifies the contributions to be made by the employer and perhaps also by the employee. These funds are then invested. The funds that accumulate are usually used at the time of retirement to purchase a retirement annuity (*i.e.*, monthly income payments). The risk that the resulting retirement income is inadequate is borne by the employee. The employee also bears the risk that investment rates of return will vary from those expected.

Table 5.2 shows the breakdown of pension plans in 1982, using this criterion. Thus, while 57.6 percent of plans were defined benefit plans, 93.7 percent of workers belonged to defined benefit plans in 1982.

Defined Benefit Versus Defined Contribution Plans

The above data indicate a significant preference in favour of defined benefit pension plans. The Allenvest Group poll (1985) found that of those who were currently participants in a pension plan, 65 percent preferred defined benefit plans, while only 28 percent preferred defined contribution plans.

Early employer-sponsored plans (such as those for the federal public service) were frequently established on a money purchase (defined contribution) basis. Over time, however, the inadequacies of such arrangements became apparent (see below). Most major plans were therefore converted to a defined benefit basis. Unions have actively bargained for defined benefit pension plans.

Defined benefit pension plans provide a more effective means of achieving particular targets of income replacement than defined contribution plans. The defined benefit plan guarantees a pension calculated on a formula based on salary and years of service. If there isn't enough money in the fund to cover the promised pension, the employer must make up the shortfall.

The defined contribution plan specifies how much the employer and/or employee contributes each year. The amount of pension remains vague until retirement, when accumulated funds are used to buy an annuity.

In a defined contribution plan, the size of the fund will depend on the investment skills of the fund manager and the values of the stocks and bonds in the fund at the time of retirement. Hence, the timing of retirement can significantly affect one's retirement income. Moreover, the cost of the retirement annuity will vary with prevailing interest rates. A person who retires when interest rates are relatively high will receive a larger annuity than a person who retires when interest rates are low. These two factors mean that such plans create a substantial level of risk for the person nearing retirement age. Over the past decade, we have experienced variations of more than 50 percent in the retirement income that could be purchased by a defined contribution scheme.

AUGUSTANA UNIVERSITY COLLEGE
LIBRARY

Unlike defined benefit plans, money purchase (defined contribution) plans place the investment risk on the employee. Particularly for large employers, it is probably more appropriate for the plan sponsor to bear the investment risk, since they can more readily adjust for fluctuations.

In summary, defined contribution plans do not provide for continuity of income (one of our income security goals) as well as defined benefit plans.

5.4 THE IMPORTANCE OF PRIVATE PENSIONS TO THE ECONOMY

The importance of private pension plans to the Canadian economy is illustrated, in Table 5.3.

TABLE 5.3

PENSION PLAN CONTRIBUTIONS, 1982

Program	# of Contributors	Total Annual Contributions (in billions)
C/QPP	10,722,472	$4.6
Employer-sponsored pension plans*	4,564,623	10.5
RRSPs	2,329,201	5.0

*includes non-contributory plan members.

Source: Statistics Canada 1984a, *Pension Plans in Canada, 1982,* 9.

The total reserves in private plans in Canada represent nearly $120 billion, or 25.9 percent of the Gross National Product (International Social Security Association 1984, 84). While most of the $4.6 billion of C/QPP contributions would be paid out immediately as benefits, the $15 billion of private source contributions are available for investment in Canada.

5.5 PENSION REFORM

The Need for Reform

Until the 1960s, pensions were viewed as a reward for long and loyal service granted out of generosity by the employer. Over the past 20 years, pensions have come to be viewed as an integral part of the total compensation package. Pension plans are expected to satisfy a variety of social needs and are now regarded as "deferred income." Unions bargain for compensation packages where hourly pay increases for active workers will be traded-off for increased pension benefits. Thus, the "deferred wage" concept has found broad, though not universal, acceptance.

With the change in attitude toward pensions, many aspects consistent with "the reward for long and loyal service" perspective came under attack. They include the following:

Gaps in Coverage

Many workers did not qualify for private pension plan coverage. Part-time workers were virtually never covered by private plans and women had less coverage than men.

Vesting and Portability

Vesting is the right of the employee to have credit for the contributions made on his or her behalf by the employer. Historically, vesting of these benefits required a worker to be age 45 **and** to have 10 years of credited service. **Portability** refers to the rights of the worker to transfer his/her pension credits from one job to the next. There was no formal mechanism allowing for, or requiring, the transfer of credited benefits from one plan to another. The importance of vesting and portability has increased with the changing labour force.

> If the labour force were stable, the vesting and portability problems would not seriously weaken the private pension system. The fact is, however, that Canada has an increasingly mobile work force. A recent study found that the average Canadian male employee works full-time for six different employers during his career. The Royal Commission on the Status of Pensions in Ontario conducted a survey which showed that women are even less apt to have the kind of work history — an uninterrupted career with one employer — required to receive a full pension upon retirement; women often leave the labour force after their first job to raise young children; spend three times longer than men between jobs; and tend to work for a shorter period than men for each employer (National Council of Welfare 1984b, 49).

Level of Employer Contributions

Under a defined benefit contributory pension plan, there are three sources of growth for the fund: employer contributions, employee contributions, and investment income. Employee contributions are defined in advance, and the balance is a mix of employer contributions and investment income. During the years 1982 to 1987, investment returns were relatively high, which allowed employers to make very small or no contributions. In some cases, employers even asked for a "refund of surplus funds." The ownership of pension fund surplus (*i.e.*, does the surplus belong to the plan sponsor or the plan participants) has been a controversial issue which has not been resolved by pension reform legislation to date.

Loss of Benefits at Death

The normal benefit at death before retirement in many private plans has been the return of the employee's contributions (usually with interest). Under the majority of private sector plans no protection was granted to the surviving spouse on the worker's death after retirement. In 1982, 87 percent of members in public sector private plans had some form of automatic survivor pension, while only 36 percent of members of private pension plans had this provision (Statistics Canada 1984a, 46, 81).

Most private pension plans that do not offer automatic survivor's benefits allow retiring members to take a reduced pension in return for continuing benefits to their surviving spouse. However, as few as one in ten choose this option (National Council of Welfare 1984b, 56). This constitutes one of the main causes of poverty among women after their husband's death.

Retirement Age

Traditionally, private pension plans specified precisely when an employee was entitled to retire and draw a full pension. There was little or no flexibility in retirement age, which was mandatory at age 65.

Indexation of Benefits

Indexation of pension benefits to maintain purchasing power has been a volatile issue. Indexation is more important for women because of their longer expected lifetime. Many pensions adjust for inflation prior to retirement, because the pension benefit is based on one's final, or final average, salary. However, relatively few plans adjust pension benefits for inflation after retirement. Presently, most federal government employees, provincial public servants, teachers, and federal members of parliament have pension benefits that are indexed to the cost of living. In the private sector, retired workers often get ad hoc (non-automatic, non-guaranteed) pension increases, but private sector employers have refused to sign a blank cheque to cover the unknown cost of future inflation.

In a 1987 survey of major Canadian employers, Hewitt Associates (1987) found that 76 percent of employers with defined benefit plans had granted at least one post-retirement pension increase during 1977-86. Of the employers who granted an increase, 52 percent granted four or more increases during 1977-86. Ninety-one percent of larger employers granted increases, compared with 62 percent of smaller employers. Canadian companies granted more increases more often than subsidiaries of U.S.-based companies. Median increases granted over the period 1977-88 represented 27 percent of the rise in the CPI. During 1982-86, increases granted replaced 43 percent of the cost of living increase; and over the last 3 years of the period of analysis, the median total increase covered one-half the rise in CPI.

In the same period, 1977-86, only 17 percent of employers with defined contribution plans granted an increase in the benefits payable.

As for automatic indexation, 66 percent of public sector plan members have automatic indexation (47 percent receiving full indexation) while only 5.4 percent of private sector plan members have automatic indexation (Statistics Canada 1984a, 48).

Even at an inflation rate as low as 4 percent per annum, the purchasing power of a fixed pension is halved every 18 years, which is less than female life expectancy at age 65. If an employee had retired in 1965, with a monthly income of $1000, the purchasing power of that pension by 1985 would have been equal to $261 (in 1965 dollars). Someone retiring in 1980 with a $1000 benefit would have seen its value decrease to $634 by 1985 (Task Force on Inflation Protection 1988, Report, 5). Even with pension adjustments equal to 40 percent of CPI increases, representing a relatively generous private sector plan, the purchasing power of the 1965 pension would still be only $441 in 1985 (Task Force on Inflation Protection 1988, Report, 5).

Thus, inflation is a serious concern to all Canadians living on a fixed income. However, the base of our income support systems, namely, OAS + GIS + C/QPP, is fully indexed to the cost of living, so that at least basic security is assured.

Pension Reform Legislation

On May 23, 1985, the federal government introduced pension reform legislation that was expected to be the model for uniform provincial legislation (except for federally regulated employment, pensions are a provincial matter). Unfortunately, reform consensus was not achieved, and each province has slightly different legislation. This makes the design and administration of pension plans difficult for companies having employees in more than one province. Most of the following changes were adopted by the provinces January 1, 1988.

Coverage

Every full-time employee who belongs to a class of employees for whom a pension plan is provided is eligible to become a member after two years of service. Part-time workers who earn at least 35 percent of the YMPE (Yearly Maximum Pensionable Earnings under the CPP, which is approximately the Average Industrial Wage) or $9,695 in 1989, in each of two consecutive years must be allowed to join if they are in the same category as full-time members (or if they worked at least 700 hours in each of two consecutive years).

The use of RRSPs was expanded to allow employees of small employers to accumulate pensions equivalent to those now available only to employees of larger firms (see Section 6.5).

Vesting and Portability

Vesting and locking-in of contributions will occur after two years of plan membership. A member with vested benefits can transfer the commuted value to another pension plan or to a prescribed savings arrangement (*e.g.*, certain RRSPs).

Minimum Employer Cost

Employers will have to pay at least 50 percent of the cost of benefits, or index deferred benefits either to 75 percent of the cost of living increase, less one percent, or to the fund's earned interest rate, less 5 percent.

Benefits at Death

If a plan member dies before retirement, the death benefit is either a lump sum to the beneficiary or an annuity to the spouse equal to the value of the member's pension credits at the time of death. For death after retirement, any member who is married at retirement must take the pension in a form that provides at least a 60 percent pension to the surviving spouse. This form of pension is automatic but can be waived if both spouses sign a waiver form. The pension to the worker can be adjusted to reflect the value of the continuing benefit to the surviving spouse.

Retirement Age

Pensionable age is the earliest age at which an unreduced pension is payable. Members must be permitted to retire up to 10 years prior to pensionable age, but benefits may be appropriately reduced. Members who postpone retirement and do not take their pension must be allowed to continue to build up credits.

Defined benefit plans are capable of providing full, or only partly reduced, benefits on early retirement. It is almost impossible, however, for defined contribution plans to give early retirement benefits that do not reflect the full actuarial reduction in benefits.

Miscellaneous Issues

Pension benefits for men and women retiring in equal circumstances must be equal. Contributions paid by employees must also be equal, but employer contributions may vary by sex. The latter variance may be necessary for plans which buy retirement annuities from life insurance companies, because such annuities cost more for women than for men, based on life expectancies.

Disclosure

Increased disclosure of pension plan information to plan members and their spouses will be required. First, material describing the plan must be provided when you are hired or at least 30 days before you are eligible to join the plan. You must be informed of any plan amendments. Additional material must be made available to you on request (*e.g.,* investment results). Moreover, regular statements will be provided showing where you stand personally with respect to your position in the plan. (*e.g.,* benefit credits earned to date).

Outstanding Issues

Indexation: The federal government did not legislate mandatory inflation protection. Instead it called for voluntary inflation protection. Ontario has recently introduced legislation to mandate inflation protection in private pensions. The legislation recommends a pension indexation formula whereby benefits would rise by 75 percent of the CPI increase, less one percent. For example, if inflation were running at eight percent a year, pension benefits would have to be increased by five percent. Adjustments would not include any CPI increases in excess of eight percent, although these adjustments might be carried forward to be taken in a year when inflation was lower. The indexation would only apply to benefits earned in the future, but there would be inducements to employers to make retroactive adjustments. Also, the protection ceases for benefits in excess of $16,620 (in 1989 dollars). Defined contribution plans will not be subject to mandatory inflation protection. It remains to be seen if other provinces will follow the Ontario lead, and if so, if this level of inflation protection will truly produce economic security.

Mandatory Retirement: Pension reform legislation mandated flexible retirement but did not address the issue of mandatory retirement (*i.e.,* the ability of an employer to force an employee to retire at a specific age). Three provinces, New Brunswick, Quebec, and Manitoba, have banned mandatory retirement. The federal government is at present abolishing mandatory retirement in areas where it has jurisdiction.

The Ontario Task Force on Mandatory Retirement (1987) published its report in December 1987. According to the report, a decision to ban mandatory retirement would affect relatively few employees, and it is not considered a pressing issue. Referring to the provinces which ban mandatory retirement, the report states:

> In all three cases the ban appears not to have had much effect on retirement practices. The proportion of the total labour force working past 65 in all three provinces has remained less than one percent, a level in line with the earlier estimates for Ontario. The trend, as in Ontario, is towards earlier rather than later retirement (Ontario Task Force on Mandatory Retirement 1987, 25).

In other words, the present trend to earlier retirement means that the abolition of mandatory retirement will have minimal impact. Unions have supported mandatory retirement to create openings in the workforce. In the future, however, business may wish to keep older workers in the labour force, since there will be fewer younger workers to fill the positions. This matter may be resolved by the Supreme Court of Canada, since several groups have challenged mandatory retirement as being in conflict with the Charter of Rights and Freedoms.

5.6 TAX REFORM

At the same time as it introduced pension reform, the federal government also introduced proposals for tax reform relevant to private pension plans and RRSPs.

Through tax reform, the government is attempting to correct three perceived shortcomings in the existing system:

(i)   There is unequal access to tax assistance for workers in different employment situations because the tax incentives differ between employees and self-employed and between defined benefit pension plans and defined contribution (money purchase) arrangements.

(ii) There is rigidity in the timing of retirement savings. Generally, contributions must be made in particular years, or the tax advantage is lost. That is, if you do not take advantage of a tax-deductible contribution in a particular year, that opportunity is gone forever.

(iii) Dollar limits on tax-deductible contributions and on tax-assisted benefits are not adjusted for inflation. In particular, the amounts that may be contributed to defined contribution (money purchase) plans have fallen behind, relative to average wages.

In short, prior to tax reform there were tax incentives that favoured the use of defined benefit plans for employer-sponsored pensions versus defined contribution arrangements (including RRSPs). Given the previously noted advantages of defined benefit plans, this may have been fortunate and intentional. Nevertheless, the federal government has decided that all forms of private pension schemes (including RRSPs) should operate on a "level playing field" when it comes to tax incentives (see Section 6.5 for details).

5.7 CONCLUSIONS

Many pension reform issues are of particular importance to women. Pension reform should, therefore, benefit women more than men. Examples include reform legislation relevant to coverage for part-time employment, earlier vesting of pension benefits, easier portability of benefits from plan to plan (women often have to move to accommodate the needs of their spouses), elimination of sex discrimination, and enhanced survivorship benefits.

Two outstanding issues also affect women more than men: indexation, given that women live longer than men; and mandatory retirement, since women may need to work beyond age 65 in order to accumulate full pension credits if they enter the workforce late in order to raise a family or because of the death of a spouse.

Another issue is the relative advantage the government intends to provide for defined benefit pension plans compared with defined contribution plans. Presently, 93.7 percent of plan members belong to defined benefit plans, primarily because defined benefit plans were historically afforded certain tax advantages.

Virtually all the pension reform legislation creates increased costs and increased administrative problems for defined benefit plans. On the other hand, few of the amendments have any effect, either as to cost or administrative difficulty, on defined contribution (money purchase) plans which leads many observers to predict a shift away from defined benefit plans toward defined contribution plans.

> The number of defined contribution pension plans more than doubled in the four years 1982 to 1986, according to figures recently released by Statistics Canada. This confirms predictions that there would be a major swing from defined benefit to defined contribution (money purchase) pension plans as a consequence of recent legislation and proposed tax changes affecting pension plans. Generally these changes will bear more heavily on defined benefit plans, especially the inflation protection proposals in Ontario. The number of defined contribution pension plans rose from 6,108 in 1982 to 12,637 in 1986 although most of them were quite small; they have an average membership of 26 and only cover 7 percent of the total membership. The number of defined benefit pension plans decreased (by 6 percent) but the membership of this type was practically unchanged. Evidently, large employers are staying with their defined benefit plans, except in a few isolated cases, but more large employers may be inclined to switch as the full implications of pension reform are appreciated. By contrast, many small employers have been switching to defined contribution plans and nearly all new pension plans are on this basis (Mercer's Bulletin 1988).

Defined benefit plans are better in terms of providing economic security than defined contribution plans, since one's replacement ratio at retirement can be predicted only under defined benefit schemes. If economic security for the elderly in Canada is a goal of society, then the possible decline of defined benefit plans should be the subject of further debate.

As the Task Force on Inflation Protection for Employment Pension Plans (1988, Report, 259) stated: "We also wish to encourage the growth of defined benefit plans. In our opinion, the defined benefit plan has certain major advantages to employees."

In summary, private pension plans ensure the income replacement level necessary to make up the difference between the actual needs of retirees and the basic protection offered under the public plans. Population aging will increase the importance of private pension plans.

> Governments are aware that the aging of the population, a demographic phenomenon we are now witnessing, will result in a noticeable cost increase for the existing public plans. It is important to enhance the role of private plans as a means of providing replacement income at retirement, if prohibitive social assistance costs are to be avoided in the future. (International Social Security Association 1987, 87).

Government-sponsored plans are funded on a "pay-as-you-go" system, which means that their cost will rise with population aging (see Section 8.2). Employer-sponsored plans, however, are fully funded in that each worker has assets backing his or her promised benefits. Such plans are immune from external demographic shifts such as the Baby Boom. In that sense, they provide a more secure basis for one's retirement income.

CHAPTER 6

INDIVIDUAL SAVINGS/REGISTERED RETIREMENT SAVINGS PLANS

6.1 INTRODUCTION

Retirement economic security requires two factors: a basic floor of income and a consistent standard of living. OAS and GIS provide a basic floor of income. C/QPP and private pension plans exist to provide a consistent standard of living. It has been noted that for the working poor and the unemployable, the government-sponsored income security schemes will replace 100 percent, or more, of pre-retirement income. For those consistently earning the Average Industrial Wage, government-sponsored schemes replace close to 40 percent of one's final earnings (14 percent from OAS and 25 percent from C/QPP). There are also funds from GIS, if needed.

When all sources of retirement income are considered, it would not be uncommon for someone who has been employed continuously and has not changed employers often to retire with a total retirement income (all sources) amounting to between 50 and 80 percent of one's salary in the last year of active employment.

The percentage ratio that one's retirement income bears to one's final salary is called one's replacement ratio (see also Sections 3.8 and 4.7). Each individual, or couple, will have a unique target replacement ratio to satisfy perceived economic security. The working poor will require 100 percent (or more) replacement of earnings just to achieve a level of income above the poverty line. The higher one's income, the lower the required replacement ratio can be in order to achieve a consistent standard of living (see Section 6.2). Regardless, one should establish a target replacement ratio and determine what proportion of that target will be satisfied by government-sponsored and employer-sponsored benefits. Any shortfall must be satisfied through individual savings.

6.2 REPLACEMENT RATIOS — AN ILLUSTRATION[1]

To determine one's target replacement ratio, one should provide answers to the following questions, stated as a percentage of present salary.

1. What work-related expenses will decline or cease at the time of retirement?
   a) all group benefit contributions
      - pension plan
      - health plan
   b) commuting costs including the cost of one's car
   c) restaurant meals, entertainment, memberships
   d) clothes and related costs
   e) union or association dues
2. What government-related expenses will cease either at retirement, or at a specified age (*e.g.*, 65)?
   a) C/QPP contributions
   b) taxes not paid as a result of reduced income
   c) health insurance premiums
3. What personal costs will end at the time of retirement or nearby?
   a) expenses related to children
   b) mortgage costs
   c) retirement savings contributions
   d) reduced need for personal insurance

It is possible for some expenses to rise, such as the need to assume personal responsibility for extended health care costs, dental care, etc. Beyond that, one must consider one's personal goals such as travel, purchase of a Florida condominium, etc.

As noted previously (Section 5.1), depending on the answers to these questions, a target replacement ratio of between 50 and 80 percent of final salary should generally allow for no disruption in one's standard of living. It might also be noted that previous generations have been able to continue to be net savers well into their retirement years (see Section 3.5).

Assuming that a person earning the Average Industrial Wage has set a target replacement ratio of 70 percent, and government-sponsored schemes replace close to 40 percent (25 percent from C/QPP and almost 15 percent from OAS), this individual must replace 30 percent of final salary from employer-sponsored and/or individually-arranged schemes. However, what will this 30 per cent benefit cost if, for whatever reason, it is completely the responsibility of the individual?

The calculations that follow are based on the following assumptions:

- Life expectancy — Canada Life Tables 1980-82
- Marginal tax rate — 40 percent
- Annual salary increase — 5 percent
- Inflation (per annum) — 4 percent
- Rate of interest (before tax) 8 1/3 percent (*i.e.*, 5 percent after tax)

If an individual wishes to replace 30 percent of final income after tax such that retirement income will increase with the rate of inflation post-retirement and, if one uses ordinary savings vehicles (not registered), the following table indicates the percentage of salary that must be set aside each year to meet the 30 percent target.

TABLE 6.1

REQUIRED PERCENTAGE OF SALARY THAT MUST BE SAVED TO ACHIEVE 70% INTEGRATED REPLACEMENT RATIO

Sex	Age At Which Saving Starts	Age at Retirement 60	65
	25	14.1	10.2
Male	30	16.5	11.6
	35	19.8	13.6
	40	24.7	16.3
	45	32.9	20.3
	25	17.5	12.9
Female	30	20.4	14.7
	35	24.5	17.2
	40	30.6	20.6
	45	40.9	25.8

These figures show how expensive true retirement income security can be, especially if one starts late in life. However, for many persons, the ability to retire on 70 percent of final salary would result in a significant increase in *disposable* income since one can then stop saving.

One should also note how much extra it costs to retire at age 60 instead of at age 65, consistent with the reduction of 30 percent for early retirement in C/QPP benefits. There are three reasons for these cost differentials:

i)   fewer total contributions are made
ii) because benefits are payable earlier, less interest income is earned, and
iii) because benefits are payable earlier, income will be paid out longer

Hence, one should be realistic in assessing the ability to afford early retirement.

However, the government has provided special tax concessions to include employer-sponsored Registered Pension Plans and individual Registered Retirement Savings Plans (see Section 6.3 for details) to assist in attaining retirement income security.

Money contributed to a Registered Pension Plan is tax deductible (within limits) at the time of contribution. Hence, for a worker in the above example, a $1 contribution to a Registered Retirement Plan costs only $.60 directly. Also, the investment income earned on a registered plan accrues tax free until taken as income. Hence, in the example above, you earn the full 8 1/3 percent rate of return (as opposed to 5 percent after tax) during the life of the plan.

On the other hand, income from a Registered Plan is taxable at the time it is taken (hopefully at lower post-retirement rates). Even if we assume the same 40 percent marginal tax rate after retirement as before, the percentages in Table 6.1 reduce substantially, if one saves through Registered Plans (see Table 6.2).

TABLE 6.2

REQUIRED PERCENTAGE OF SALARY THAT MUST BE SAVED USING REGISTERED RETIREMENT PLANS

Sex	Age At Which Saving Starts	Age at Retirement	
		60	65
	25	6.0	4.1
Male	30	7.7	5.2
	35	10.0	6.6
	40	13.7	8.7
	45	19.9	11.8
	25	7.0	4.9
Female	30	8.9	6.2
	35	11.7	7.9
	40	16.0	10.4
	45	23.2	14.1

Table 6.2 illustrates that, for many individuals, the required savings rate is cut in half, or more, by using registered plans.

Virtually all employer-sponsored plans are registered, and much of the target replacement ratio will be satisfied in this way. To the extent that it is not, one must assume responsibility for the balance. Obviously it is advantageous to do so through registered means. These individually-arranged schemes are called Registered Retirement Savings Plans (RRSPs).

6.3 RRSPs — HISTORY

Registered Retirement Savings Plans started under amendments to the *Income Tax Act* introduced in 1957. The original legislation provided tax incentives as long as the individual then purchased a **life annuity** by age 71 (one could take the proceeds as a lump sum, but this sum would all be taxable income in one year and would thus incur a higher tax).

The amount of money that could be placed in an RRSP was increased regularly. However, contribution limits were frozen from 1976 to 1986, as follows:

- Taxpayers who were not members of a Registered Pension Plan were allowed to deduct up to $5,500 each year or 20 percent of earned income, whichever was less.
- Taxpayers who were members of a Registered Pension Plan were allowed to deduct up to $3,500 each year or 20 percent of earned income, whichever was less, minus their contributions, if any, to the employer's plan.

This tax formula was designed to give workers who were not covered by an employer-sponsored pension plan the ability to achieve some level of retirement income security.

Income that qualified and could be contributed to an RRSP was virtually all income, including pension benefits, C/QPP benefits, and OAS benefits but *not* investment income. Since, at the inception of RRSPs, C/QPP benefits did not exist, and OAS benefits did not start until age 70, these extra sources of tax-exempt contributions may have been allowed through omission. The intent of RRSPs is to level one's lifetime income. You defer income (and income tax) during your working years and then take that income (and pay tax) during retirement. Investment income is not subject to such deferral since there is no reason to expect it to end at the time of retirement.

Workers can place their contributions (within the above limits) into a spousal RRSP. This is often advantageous if the spouse is not earning income or pension credits, since the spouse's income tax bracket after retirement would frequently be lower than that of the retired worker. It also provides an incentive to provide retirement income security to the dependent spouse.

Until 1978, the only form of retirement income that one could purchase from an RRSP was an annuity payable for life. This annuity could have a guaranteed period and could be designed to continue payments to the surviving spouse (last survivor annuity). The more guarantees included, the lower the initial income one receives per unit of RRSP fund.

On April 10, 1978, the government introduced two extra maturity options. The first was an annuity-certain (*i.e.*, payments do not depend on one's continued survivorship) payable to age 90, and the second was a special payout scheme called a Registered Retirement Income Fund (RRIF). It is not the purpose of this monograph to describe these options in detail, but the elderly should investigate these options before committing their life savings (see Delaney 1987).

The rules governing RRIFs have been liberalised over the years so that one can tailor one's income to needs (as long as one withdraws a minimum amount each year and pays income tax on the amount withdrawn). For example, a person wishing to retire at age 60, but unable to receive a company pension until age 65, can take heavier withdrawals from the RRIF for five years and then cut back. Also, one can withdraw larger amounts for emergencies. There is no problem with an RRIF of being forced to buy an annuity when interest rates are low. However, all RRIF funds must be withdrawn (and tax paid) by age 90.

The advantage of the RRIF is its flexibility. The only restriction on the RRIF is that, after age 71, there is a defined minimum withdrawal each year (which is taxable income) that will exhaust the fund by age 90. Beyond that, the fund holder is free to do almost anything. Withdrawals need not be level; funds can be self-directed as to their investment; withdrawals can be tailored to provide inflation protection.

The disadvantage of the RRIF and the annuity-certain to age 90 is that they are formulated to provide income only to age 90. Given that 29 percent of women aged 71 and 14 percent of men aged 71 will survive beyond age 90 (Statistics Canada 1984b), there should exist serious concern about the ability of the average retiree to comprehend this possible source of income inadequacy. The ability to provide lifetime income security is the main advantage of the life annuity.

RRSPs represent a defined contribution (money purchase) pension plan. One makes contributions which grow with earned investment income. As one approaches age 71, one buys an annuity or a pay-out RRIF. As with other defined contribution pension plans, the interest rate prevailing at the time of purchase of the retirement income annuity will vary with the prevailing interest rates. Hence, one is well-advised not to wait until age 71 to buy the income annuity, in case interest rates decrease just when one is forced to buy. For example, in September 1987, when interest rates were in the 10 to 11 percent range, a $50,000 lump sum could buy a straight life annuity (no guaranteed period) paying $583 a month for a 65-year-old male. An annuity with a 10-year guarantee paid $543 a month; with a 15-year guarantee, $522 a month (*The Financial Post, Moneywise Magazine* 1988, 89). A typical last-survivor annuity with payments continuing to the surviving spouse, covering two 65-year-olds, and with a 10-year guaranteed period, paid $492 a month. Payments to individual female recipients are lower because of their longer life expectancy.

6.4 THE IMPORTANCE OF RRSPs TO THE ECONOMY

Table 6.3 shows the contributions made to RRSPs by Canadian taxpayers in 1985.

TABLE 6.3
CONTRIBUTIONS TO RRSPs 1987

Income Level $	Number of Contributors	Proportion of Tax Filers %	Total $ Contributions (,000)	Average $ Contribution
0-5,000	20,590	0.9	10,622	516
5-10,000	100,320	3.7	100,139	998
10-15,000	256,850	11.2	363,578	1,416
15-20,000	364,810	18.6	641,945	1,760
20-25,000	446,650	26.6	922,099	2,064
25-30,000	438,740	32.9	980,563	2,235
30-40,000	787,590	40.4	1,957,047	2,485
40-50,000	514,370	49.7	1,444,860	2,809
50,000 and over	553,600	57.8	2,603,068	4,702
Total	3,483,650	20.4	9,024,445	2,591

SOURCE: Revenue Canada, *Taxation Statistics for 1987*, 1989 Edition

Table 6.3 shows that RRSPs are used more by the wealthy, for several reasons. First, the poor do not have the disposable income to direct toward RRSPs. Second, the tax incentives that encourage the use of RRSPs are of little or no value to the poor, but are of increasing value as one's income rises. Third, those receiving the federal GIS/SPA or provincial Supplements will have any RRSP income "taxed back" at marginal rates of 50 to 100 percent (see Sections 4.4/4.5). Finally, government-sponsored pension plans (see Figure 4.1) will replace more than 100 percent of pre-retirement net income for the poor, but less than 30 percent of net income to the relatively wealthy. Thus, RRSPs are not designed to provide a minimum income security floor, but mainly provide security in maintaining one's standard of living.

These savings also provide an important source of investable funds for the economy. In 1969, fewer than 206,000 individuals contributed an average of $867 per person to RRSPs. By 1983, 2.3 million Canadians contributed to RRSPs, and the average annual contribution was $2,145 (Task Force on Inflation Protection 1988, Report, 22). Total net annual RRSP contributions have risen from $27.5 million in 1960 to $225 million in 1970 and $3.7 billion in 1980. By 1983, net annual contributions climbed to nearly $5 billion even though RRSP contribution limits were frozen from 1976 to 1986 (Task Force on Inflation Protection 1988, Report, 22). The 1987 total contribution was $9 billion (see Table 6.3). As of February 29, 1988, the deadline for 1987 RRSP contributions, it was estimated that there was a total of $85 billion invested in RRSPs. RRSPs account for 8 percent of total savings, up from less than 1 percent in 1970 (Task Force on Inflation Protection, Vol. 2. 1988, 47). These funds represent an important source of risk capital for the economy.

6.5 TAX REFORM

Tax reform for pensions was introduced to allow equitable treatment for all retirement income security savings plans (see Section 5.6). Prior to tax reform, workers not participating in employer-sponsored pension plans could not achieve the same level of retirement savings through RRSPs because of the relatively low contribution limits (see Section 6.3 of this chapter).

Under the 1990 tax reform legislation, by 1995, someone who is not a member of an employer-sponsored pension plan will be able to contribute up to the lesser of $15,500, or 18 percent of earned income, to an RRSP. After 1995, the $15,500 limit will be indexed to the rise in the Average Industrial Wage so as to retain its real value.

If one participates in an employer-sponsored plan, the 18 percent/ $15,500 limit will be reduced by something called a "pension adjustment," which is the "value" of the contribution to the employer-sponsored pension plan. If that plan is a defined contribution plan, it will be the total contribution made (employer plus employee). If it is a defined benefit plan, it will be nine times the amount of increased benefit in that year. For example, if the benefit is 1.5 percent per year of service, the pension adjustment will be 13.5 percent (9 times 1.5) and the maximum allowable contribution to an RRSP will be 4.5 percent of earnings.

Also, under tax reform, one will no longer be able to roll over pension income tax-free into an RRSP. This includes Old Age Security (OAS), Canada/Quebec Pension Plan (C/QPP) benefits, as well as other pension income. This is consistent with the "deferred wage" concept of tax-encouraged pension plan contributions, since the three sources of income listed above do not cease until death. In addition, under tax reform, if it is not possible to contribute the entire allowable amount to your RRSP, any "deficiency" can be carried forward up to seven years. The best advice remains to contribute as early as possible, however, to earn the maximum possible tax-sheltered interest.

Based on public opinion polls, this expansion of RRSPs should be popular. In the poll (Allenvest Group Limited 1985) referred to previously, Canadians were asked if they would rather contribute to a government-sponsored plan or some personal retirement scheme (*e.g.*, RRSP). Sixty-one percent reported a greater preference for the personal plan, with 36 percent favouring the government-sponsored plan. When given the choice between contributing to an employer-sponsored plan or to a personal scheme, 58 percent preferred a personal plan, with 33 percent preferring an employer-sponsored plan. A breakdown of the responses showed that respondents already in a company pension plan showed a greater preference for employer-sponsored plans.

Also, when those surveyed were asked if they were worried about receiving their plan benefits, 31 percent said yes for GIS; 44 percent worried about OAS; 42 percent about C/QPP; 31 percent about employer-sponsored plans; while only 19 percent showed concern over their RRSP, and 28 percent over personal assets. On all items, women were more likely to be concerned than men (Allenvest Group Limited 1985). Hence, there is an enhanced feeling of economic security when the funds are controlled by the individual.

However, RRSPs represent a defined contribution (money purchase) form of pension plan with all its inherent disadvantages (see Section 5.7). With the expansion of tax concessions for RRSPs, we can expect a continuation of the switch to defined contribution plans (including group RRSPs), especially among small employers, with the implications outlined in Chapter 5.

6.6 REVERSE MORTGAGES

Chapter 3 showed that there is a great disparity of wealth among elderly Canadians. In many cases, especially with elderly women, individuals are income poor but asset rich. That is, many elderly women have income levels that place them below the poverty line, but are living in houses that are mortgage free.

One solution that may prove to be popular is the "reverse mortgage." These plans allow seniors to convert some of the value of their home into retirement income. The financial institution providing the income holds a mortgage against the house that is equal in value to the retirement income paid out. The mortgage so created is paid off when the retiree dies or sells the house. Monthly payments from the annuity are not taxable, and do not affect a homeowner's eligibility for income supplements (*e.g.*, GIS). While similar plans have long been popular in England and Europe, to date these schemes have only found a narrow market in Canada and the United States.

6.7 CONCLUSIONS

This chapter analysed the tax-encouraged form of individual retirement savings; namely, the Registered Retirement Savings Plan. While there is a large variety of savings vehicles, Section 6.2, Replacement Ratios, showed that registered savings plans are the most efficient form of savings because of their tax advantages. The key is to plan carefully, and start one's savings program early.

As noted in Section 5.7, employer-sponsored pension plans are not affected by the aging of the population. The same is true for individual savings, including RRSPs. Each individual has real assets backing the account to its full stated value.

The two requirements for economic security are a basic floor of guaranteed income plus the maintenance of one's standard of living. Chapter 4 described how OAS plus GIS provide Canadians with a floor of guaranteed income. C/QPP along with employer-sponsored pension plans (Chapter 5) and individual schemes (Chapter 6) are essential ingredients in achieving the other attribute of economic security, a consistent standard of living.

NOTE

1 The calculations shown are only approximations and may not be reproduced exactly in reality.

CHAPTER 7

ECONOMIC SECURITY ASPECTS
OF HEALTH CARE

7.1 INTRODUCTION

The foundation of the Canadian income security system is government-sponsored social security made up of OAS, GIS, and C/QPP. While C/QPP is funded by defined contributions, OAS and GIS are dependent upon general tax revenues. Any segment of government spending where costs are escalating beyond the growth in tax revenues, for example, health care, could threaten the continued security provided by OAS and GIS.

Canadians are told they have a good health care system, but doubts persist.

> By world standards, Canada has a first class health care system. Access is virtually universal (and prompt to boot); facilities are widely available; the quality of care is good; costs are reasonable; and techniques, up-to-date. But Canadians themselves tend to be critical of their system, with many calling for major reforms (Economic Council of Canada 1987b, 2).

This chapter will show that health care costs are presently rising more rapidly than Gross National Product. The chapter will also show how an aging population, of and by itself, will create its own cost-escalation pressures. The chapter will go on to show possible ways for a more economical delivery of health care services so as to allow for manageable increases in health care costs. If these reforms are forthcoming, Canada's health care delivery system need not threaten the economic security of the aging population.

7.2 THE HISTORY OF HEALTH CARE FUNDING
IN CANADA

In Canada, health care comes primarily under provincial jurisdiction. Hence, it took time, and political ingenuity, for a national health care delivery system to evolve. Even so, there are still significant provincial variations in both benefits and financing.

The first federal intervention was the National Health Grants Programme of 1948, which was intended to overcome perceived shortages of health resources after the Depression and war. A universal coverage hospital insurance plan already existed in Saskatchewan (1946), followed by British Columbia (1949). These provincial schemes appeared to result in both greater equity of access to services and better control of costs than the systems, in other provinces, which were made up of industry pre-payment plans combined with government subsidies to assist persons unable to pay (International Social Security Association 1983b, 17).

In 1957, the federal government introduced the *Hospital Insurance and Diagnostic Services Act,* S.C. 1957, c. 28, whereby the federal government would pay approximately 50 percent of the cost of provincial health care plans that qualified under defined criteria. By 1961, all provinces and territories had joined the national program, which focussed on pre-payment of hospital in-patient care and diagnostic services. This was followed by the *Medical Care Act,* S.C. 1966-67, c. 64, which added universal coverage of physician services from 1968. All provinces and territories joined the medical care arrangements by 1972.

Because of a concern that there was no incentive for the provinces to control costs, new funding arrangements were legislated in 1977 (the *Federal-Provincial Fiscal Arrangements and Established Programmes Financing Act 1977,* S.C. 1976-77, c. 10 or EPF). Instead of the federal government paying (approximately) 50 percent of the cost, payments from the federal government are now composed of an increased transfer of tax revenues and special cash grants. As a result of this Act, federal contributions, in general, will rise with GNP. This places the responsibility for controlling health care costs, beyond the rise in GNP, solely on the provinces. Along with the EPF arrangement, the federal government granted conditional support for nursing home care, residential care for adults, health aspects of home care, and ambulatory health care services. The motivation for this federal intervention was not just the goal of establishing a national health care system.

> The money was provided, not because the federal government was inter-
> ested in creating national standards for extended health care programmes
> but to meet provincial criticisms that federal funding encouraged provinces
> to adopt high cost solutions to health and aging problems, specifically by
> utilizing hospitals rather than nursing homes (Brown, M. 1987, 31).

In the early 1980s, the federal government became concerned that certain of the original basic standards, such as universal access, were being eroded. In particular, they objected to some provinces allowing hospitals to charge user fees and doctors to extra-bill. Their answer was the *Canada Health Act,* S.C. 1984, c. 6, which imposed financial penalties on provinces that did not allow reasonable access to health services without financial or other barriers. By late 1980, all provinces had passed legislation eliminating extra-billing and user fees.

Each province and territory has its own method of paying its part of the costs. Two provinces, Alberta and British Columbia, require premium payments by participants. In Alberta, residents aged 65 and over (and their dependents) do not pay premiums. These two provinces subsidize low income residents. Ontario, Quebec, and Manitoba use a payroll tax, payable by employers, to partly fund their health care schemes. All other provinces finance their plans through general tax revenues.

As to variance in benefits, prescription drug plans are found in all provinces and territories except Prince Edward Island. Dental-care plans for the elderly exist in Alberta and the Yukon. Hearing aids are covered benefits in British Columbia, Saskatchewan, and Alberta. In the area of long-term care, several provinces have insured nursing home care, while others have not (Economic Council of Canada 1987b, 19). Other provincial variations exist (see Marshall 1987, 509).

The introduction of government funding caused health care costs to rise.

Not surprisingly, the introduction of comprehensive public insurance in Canada between 1956 and 1971 increased expenditures on hospital and medical services significantly. Measured in terms of 1971 dollars per capita, expenditures increased from $1,141 in 1956 to $4,403 in 1971, representing an average growth rate of 9.42 percent. While over half of this growth was financed rather painlessly through growth in real GNP, it nevertheless also represented a trend toward increasing tax burdens for Canadians (Brown, M. 1987, 32).

However, since 1971, health spending in Canada has not risen as rapidly as in most other Western developed countries (International Social Security Association 1983b, 17). This is illustrated in Figure 7.1. Hence, there is no basis to argue that government funding is the cause of growing health care costs. This is discussed in more detail in Section 7.6.

The effect of the introduction of medicare has been studied by Enterline, Salter, McDonald, and McDonald (Brown, M. 1987) who investigated the effect of medicare on the demand for physician care in the Montreal area (1969-70 versus 1971-72). They found that the quantity of care demanded did not change. However, analysis by income level showed increased demand by lower income groups and decreased demand by higher income groups.

The increased utilization by the poor was an expected effect of introducing public insurance, but the decreased utilization by the rich was not. One way of explaining the statistics is by postulating that, in the post-medicare period, waiting time replaced money as the major cost incurred by consumer-patients in acquiring care (Pifer and Bronte 1986, 62).

What characterizes the history of medicare legislation in Canada is that the purpose of the system is to pay the bills. To date, governments have

Figure 7.1
Hospital and Physicians' Expenses
As a Share of GNP for Canada and the U.S 1948-85.

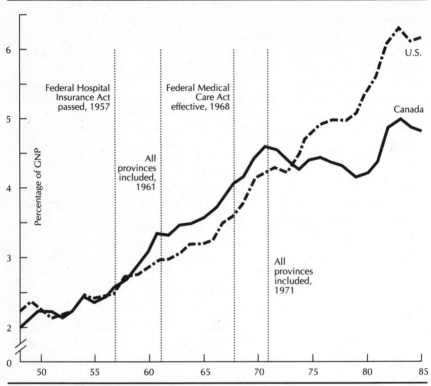

Source: Evans 1987, 170.

not exerted much in the way of external management control. "Governments replaced private insurers but did not pretend to run health services. This self-denying ordinance on the part of governments was the price that had to be paid to overcome the resistance of the medical profession" (Economic Council of Canada 1987b, 156).

7.3 PRESENT USE OF THE HEALTH CARE SYSTEM

Age and sex are important factors in the use of medical care resources. Table 7.1 shows the use of hospitals by age and sex.

A further breakdown of data by age shows that patient days per person

TABLE 7.1

HOSPITAL SEPARATIONS* AND DAYS OF CARE IN HOSPITAL BY AGE GROUP AND SEX, 1984-85

	Separations per 1,000 population		Days per Separation	
	Women	Men	Women	Men
Age group				
Under 1	252.9	340.4	7.2	7.0
1-4	92.6	129.4	4.5	4.2
5-14	50.2	58.5	4.7	4.9
15-19	114.4	58.5	5.1	6.9
20-24	206.0	63.3	5.0	7.6
25-34	223.6	64.8	5.6	8.0
35-44	126.2	80.0	7.6	8.5
45-64	149.0	164.7	11.4	11.2
65-74	254.0	336.2	17.6	15.9
75 and over	417.9	544.0	32.2	24.1
Total	166.6	122.6	11.2	11.7

* A separation occurs when a patient is either discharged from hospital or dies.

SOURCE: Statistic Canada *Hospital Morbidity*, 1989, Catalogue 82-206.

in Canadian general hospitals double between the ages of 65 and 75 and increase fourfold and more between 65 and 85 (Gross and Schwenger 1981, 79).

Elderly women are heavier users of the health care system than elderly men. There are several reasons for this. First, women live longer than men, and therefore more women reach the age where extended care is required. Second, elderly women are more apt to live alone (see Section 2.3). The existence of a spouse at home allows many elderly men to remain in their homes. Hence, while women account for a higher proportion of the demand for health care, they also account for a higher proportion of the supply of health care, both formal and informal (Economic Council of Canada 1987b, 21).

However, concentration on age alone may distort the ability to see possible causal effects, as demonstrated by Table 7.2, which analyses statistics on hospital usage.

While age is still a factor in the health-care-cost formula, it is not the only, and may not be the most important, factor since there is a similarity in hospital use in the last year of life regardless of age.

TABLE 7.2

HOSPITAL USAGE (AVERAGE DAYS PER YEAR)

Age	Individuals With No Deaths	Individuals Who Died Number of Years Before Death			
		4	3	2	1
25-64	1.3	6.0	7.6	7.6	23.5
65-84	3.8	7.1	9.4	10.6	32.0
85+	6.8	9.5	9.9	8.1	24.4

SOURCE: Economic Council of Canada 1987b, 53.

Scitovsky did a study in which he showed that 30 percent of all health care expenses occurred in the final 30 days of life; 46 percent in the last 60 days; and 77 percent during the last six months. Clearly, dying is a costly process (Economic Council of Canada 1987b, 109).

Also, the hospital days accounted for by the elderly may not be as expensive as for the average patient. Many of the elderly require only board, lodging, and nursing care and make no demands on expensive diagnostic and therapeutic services. Thus, bed-days may not provide a correct measure of the impact of the elderly on health care costs. In fact, the elderly who occupy acute-care hospital beds may be there solely because they are awaiting transfer to a nursing home. "In Winnipeg, a city relatively well endowed with institutional resources, the average wait for nursing home transfer in 1976 was 71.2 days. Recent Toronto data indicate much longer waiting periods, ranging from 57.1 days for residential care to 124.3 days for chronic care" (Marshall 1987, 541).

The delivery of health care is expensive, and the costs are rising.

TABLE 7.3

HEALTH EXPENDITURES IN CANADA

	1970		1985	
	$ per capita	% GNP	$ per capita	% GNP
Institutional & related services	153.03	3.81	805.63	4.43
Professional services	66.13	1.65	352.78	1.94
Drugs and appliances	36.55	0.91	194.71	1.07
Other expenses	37.67	0.94	190.13	1.05
Total	293.38	7.30	1,543.26	8.48

SOURCE: Brown, M. 1987, 3.

In Ontario, health care expenditures account for nearly one-third of total provincial expenditures (Province of Ontario 1987, 7), and costs are rising.

> The average length of stay has increased less than 1 percent annually since 1961, while costs of hospital services per patient, **net** of wages and price inflation, have increased at an annual rate of 3.3 percent (Auer 1987, 20).
>
> As Canada's population grew at an annual rate of 1.5 percent, a similar rate of increase could be expected in hospital services. Instead, the volume of services increased at an average annual rate of 5 percent (Auer 1987, 56).

Thus, population forces do not explain the rise in costs. Instead we must look at the health care delivery system itself. Various researchers argue that patients are being treated in a more costly manner.

> Among the various cost factors common to all hospital departments and services, higher hospital wage rates accounted for almost two-thirds of the overall rise in costs per patient, greater service intensity for one-quarter, and higher prices of hospital supplies for the remaining tenth ... Administrative and supportive services contributed, on average, as much or more to the rise in costs than expenditures on inpatient care of the nursing department (Economic Council of Canada 1987b, 179).

These figures mean that hospital costs have been rising faster than the increase in demand for their services. In other words, hospital "productivity" diminished over this period. Moreover, this decline in productivity has been more rapid in recent years.

> This apparent long-term decline in hospital productivity is unusual not only because it differs so much from developments in other industries but also because some of the decline may have been caused by the adoption of new technology.
>
> Historically, new industrial technology has brought improvements in productivity. The same can be said for medical technology. When antibiotics were first applied, during the 1940s and early 1950s, they reduced infectious disease, shortened hospital stays, and reduced per-patient costs.
>
> But the new and very costly treatments introduced during the 1960s and 1970s — kidney transplants, heart transplants, hip joint replacements, and double or triple heart bypasses — required more intensive care... Each of the new and more-intensive techniques of treatment has brought new excitement and hope, and also higher cost. Conservative estimates put the cost of intensive care per hospital-day at three times that of regular ward care. Evidence of the benefits is not conclusive (Auer 1987, 26).
>
> In general, it is now possible to keep sicker and sicker people alive longer and longer at greater and greater cost (Canadian Medical Association 1984, 41).

The decision to make costly technologies available to the elderly is not universally accepted. "For example, in Great Britain dialysis is not available to anyone over 55 within the national health-care system" (Wigdor and Foot 1988, 77).

However, it is not possible to find evidence of measurable health improvements that match the rate of increase in health care costs. Life expectancy, for example, has increased but not in proportion to the increase in the volume of health services provided. Additional health expenditures appear to be producing diminishing returns in measurable health improvements (Economic Council of Canada 1987b, 187). To reinforce this lack of correlation between increased health expenditures and measurable benefits, it is worth noting that health expenditures today vary among the provinces, on a per capita basis, by more than 20 percent, but life expectancy varies by only 2 percent (Economic Council of Canada 1987b, 197). These comments are reinforced by broader international comparisons.

7.4 INTERNATIONAL COMPARISON

Table 7.4 presents a brief international comparison of health care costs and indicators commonly used to measure health status for some of the world's industrialized nations.

TABLE 7.4

RESOURCE AND HEALTH INDICATOR ESTIMATES, 1983

Country	Health expenditures as % GNP	Life expectancy at birth	Infant mortality per 1,000 live births
Canada	8.6	74	10
United States	10.8	73	12
France	9.3	74	10
Britain	6.2	73	12
Japan	6.7	76	7

SOURCE: (Auer 1987, 3; and Province of Ontario 1984, 31).

This table reinforces the earlier suggestions that increased expenditures on health care do not bring commensurate increases in measurable population health attributes. The United States spends 60 percent or more on health care than Japan but has a lower population life expectancy and higher infant mortality rates (among the countries listed, Japan also has the fewest physicians per capita (Auer 1987, 1)). This comparison only presents measurable attributes of population health. Other attributes, such as quality of life, have no agreed method of measurement.

The relatively low level of spending on health care in Canada and Japan can be explained partly by the fact that their populations are relatively young. In 1985, 10 percent of the population in Canada and Japan was aged 65 and over, while the proportions in the United States and Europe are between 12 and 16 percent (see Chapter 2). However, demographically, Britain has the "oldest" population of the five countries listed, spends the lowest percent of GNP on health care, yet has measurable health indicators that are in line with other nations spending more on their health care systems. In Britain, the health care marketplace is dominated and largely controlled by the government. Expenditures on health services have not increased as rapidly as the increase in the number of elderly (Economic Council of Canada 1987b, 29). Hence, government funding and control of health care delivery do not result in increased health care costs.

The United States system is unique among the five presented in that in the U.S. 58 percent of health expenditures comes from the private sector. This widely diversified funding base has not aided cost containment. One reason may be the lack of cost containment implicit in the private-funding basis. "The concept of rationing is largely ignored. With some important exceptions, the norm for American hospital care approximates the maxim 'if it will help, do it' " (Canadian Medical Association 1984, 98).

One statistic often presented to explain differences in per capita health care costs from country to country is the rate of institutionalization, that is, the proportion of the elderly that is placed in health care facilities (*e.g.*, hospitals, nursing homes). Forbes *et al.* estimate that 8.4 percent of Canada's population aged 65 and over was institutionalized in 1976 (1987, 40). By contrast, 5.1 percent of Britain's and 6.3 percent of the United States' population aged 65 and over are found in institutions (Forbes *et al.* 1987, 43). They go on to say that this may be partly due to Canada not insuring home-care services as early as it insured hospital and institutional care; in Britain these services were insured simultaneously.

The fiscal consequences of these differences are significant. For example, in Ontario, over three-quarters of the province's health expenditures for the aged are for institutions. Ontario spends 31 percent more per capita than the United States on the institutional care of its aged (Gross and Schewenger 1981, 43). This appears to be an obvious target for attainment of health care cost savings.

Given the increased costs of health care, virtually all industrialized countries are exercising increased levels of control over medical expenditures. Some countries are controlling the expansion of hospitals and equipment, others have regulated physicians and pharmaceutical manufacturers (United States Department of Health and Human Services 1985, xxiv).

As noted, health care costs in Canada have risen more rapidly than inflation during the past two decades. While the elderly use a disproportionate share of these health care services, the general aging of the

Canadian population does not explain completely this rise in costs in excess of inflation (see Canadian Medical Association 1984). In the next section the analysis turns to the effect that an aging population has on health care costs.

7.5 POPULATION AGING — ITS EFFECT ON HEALTH CARE COSTS

Health care costs and age are highly correlated, as illustrated in Figure 7.2.

FIGURE 7.2

RELATIVE PER CAPITA COSTS OF HEALTH CARE FOR
MALES AND FEMALES BY AGE

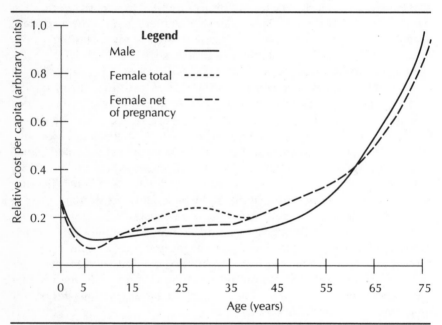

SOURCE: Marshall 1987, 555.

Given the statistics on the aging of the population as outlined in Chapter 2, it is not surprising that health care costs are expected to rise, especially since the old/old proportion of the population is growing faster than the young/old (see Chapter 2); and it is this former group that makes the largest demand on the health care system (Province of Ontario 1987, 18).

In a study completed for the Canadian Medical Association (1984)

Woods Gordon developed a model to forecast the relative magnitude of growth in the demand for major health care services, and the approximate increase in the resources required to meet that demand, given no change in our health care delivery methods (*i.e.*, only the effect of the aging population) (see Table 7.5).

TABLE 7.5

PROJECTED PERCENTAGE INCREASE
HEALTH SERVICE UTILIZATION

	1981-2001		1981-2021	
	20-year	annual	40-year	annual
General and allied special hospitals (inpatient)	48.8	2.01	89.1	1.61
Long-term care facilities	68.3	2.64	118.8	1.98
Mental health (inpatient)	38.3	1.63	68.0	1.31
Physician services	27.2	1.21	45.0	0.93
Home care (nursing visits)	62.6	2.46	117.8	1.97

SOURCE: Canadian Medical Association 1984, 14.

To explain the impact of these projected increases, the Canadian Medical Association goes on to say:

> To put this in perspective, total "public" health expenditures (that is, by governments and municipalities, excluding private spending) in 1981, excluding capital expenditures, were $18.5 billion. Thus, by the year 2021, demographic changes alone will increase current expenditures on health care by about 75 percent to over $32 billion if current patterns of providing care remain unchanged. This converts to an annual increase in current expenditures of about 1.4 percent.
>
> With respect to long-term care beds, the status quo projections would require unprecedented construction activity in this area of health care. Almost one thousand 300-bed long-term care facilities would have to be built to provide the additional beds required. As a point of reference, in 1980/81 Statistics Canada reported less than 500 facilities of 100+ beds in Canada serving the elderly population (Canadian Medical Association 1984, 17, 18).

One of the assumptions in these projections is that we can continue to deliver today's level of health care at the same cost per unit of demand as is being paid today. Is that realistic? In response, Stoddart points out that: "the age-sex specific utilization rates of 'traditional' services by the elderly, assumed constant in most projections, are in fact increasing, at the same time as the range of 'alternative' services is expanding." (Economic Council of Canada 1987b, 69).

Further, the cohort of aged that will increase the pressure on health care services in the next century is the most highly educated to date. Educational attainment is correlated with enhanced life expectancy, which may lead to increased demands on health services and corresponding higher expenditures (Gross and Schwenger 1981, 84; and Marshall 1987, 420).

Also, families are now smaller and more mobile, and more women have independent working careers which, as discussed in Section 2.5., *may* reduce the number of family caretakers (Gross and Schwenger 1981, 84; and Marshall 1987, 478) which would exacerbate the cost increase problem. Further, the new and expensive technologies available for health care application may accelerate the expansion of health care costs if we adopt the principle that everyone is entitled to the best possible standard of health care. This is especially true because of our proximity to the United States where few controls are being placed on the use of these new technologies. Hence, if people see a technology available in the U.S., there will be a tendency for them to demand that it be available in Canada.

However, the majority of researchers do not paint such a pessimistic picture, for two reasons. First, the expansion in projected costs is estimated to be 75 percent over 40 years, or 1.4 percent per annum. If our GNP continues to expand as in the past, this 1.4 percent growth will be less than GNP expansion, with the result that health care will consume no larger a proportion of GNP than today. Second, most researchers suggest that there are inefficiencies in the present system of health care delivery that can be overcome if the political will exists to do so. These issues will be reviewed in some detail in the next section.

7.6 PUBLIC POLICY ISSUES AND ALTERNATIVES

There appears to be general agreement that the aging of the Canadian population, per se, need not create a funding crisis in our health care delivery system. It is also believed that the health care delivery system is presently strongly influenced by factors other than "need," such as the availability of hospital beds, the way in which physicians practise medicine, and the number of physicians (Economic Council of Canada 1987b, 51).

Starting with the availability of hospital beds, Table 7.6 presents data on hospital bed usage that indicates that the availability of beds is an important factor in how many beds are actually used and may, therefore, *appear* to be needed.

Evans (1984, 85, 86) notes that: "Overall bed capacity emerges from study after study as the single most important factor influencing hospital inpatient utilization, and the level of bed capacity at which use would appear to stop responding to increases is double or triple current capacity or need estimates." Further, Fisher and Zorzitto (1983) state:

TABLE 7.6

HOSPITAL USAGE ACCORDING TO AVAILABILITY OF HOSPITAL BEDS IN AREA OF RESIDENCE

	Number of available hospital beds per 1,000 persons		
Age of patient	Less than 5	5-7.9	8+
25-64	2.2	2.3	3.5
65-84	7.0	8.6	9.4
85+	10.8	20.3	25.2
All 25 and over	3.0	3.9	5.2

SOURCE:Economic Council of Canada 1987b, 53.

"The very presence of the patient, even though he or she may only be awaiting transfer, can prompt investigations for the sake of completeness... The acute care medical setting encourages such patients to be passive and dependent while the necessary investigations and treatments are undertaken, since the emphasis is on diagnosis, treatment, and cure, rather than on rehabilitation."

In addition, hospitalization may actually be detrimental to the patient. "There are no data to suggest that high hospital usage practice styles are related to favourable patient outcomes. Because of the high risk of hospital acquired infections and falls in the hospitalized elderly patient, quite the opposite may be true" (Economic Council of Canada 1987b, 56).

As stated in Section 7.3, inappropriate use of acute care facilities by chronic care patients may not be the choice of the patient. Rather, it is often the unavailability of chronic care facilities, or a lack of communication within the system, which would facilitate efficient transferral. This inappropriate use of acute care facilities not only means increased costs but also provides care to the elderly that is inappropriate to their needs (McDaniel 1986, 335). "It is common for between 10 percent and 20 percent of the acute hospital beds in any Ontario city to be occupied by such patients" (Province of Ontario 1987, 8).

There may even be a slight financial incentive for the hospital in this misuse of facilities, since these patients require less expensive care than the true acute-care patient (Province of Ontario 1987, 8; and Marshall 1987, 543). What is needed, therefore, is a system that provides incentives to place patients in the level of care most appropriate to their needs and that at the same time optimizes the costs of care delivery.

The second determining factor in the consumption of health care services is the way in which physicians practise medicine.

Evans (1976) demonstrates the major role of physicians in cost figures. He estimates they control approximately 80 percent of health-care costs. Even though only about 19 percent of the total-health care expenditures in Canada go directly to physicians, this group largely controls hospital utilization (accounting for about half of all health-care costs), prescribing of drugs, etc. That is, the decision to use expensive health-care services is not made primarily by the individual patient or client. The decision is made primarily by medical doctors. They are the major gatekeepers to utilization of the system. Physicians and other providers have expert knowledge not shared by patients and make decisions on patients' behalf (Chappell *et al.* 1986, 100).

Given the level of control, physicians do not always act in the most cost-efficient manner. There are reasons for these inefficiencies.

Incentives for efficient health care delivery are particularly absent, in fact they are perverse. Fee-for-service reimbursement of physicians encourages a service-intensive-practice style. Community physicians have no incentive to make efficient use of hospitals and their technologic capacity, because hospitals represent a "free" complementary capital input. Current methods of reimbursing hospitals, which all amount to a form of cost reimbursement, neither encourage nor reward efficient institutions (Canadian Medical Association 1984, 65).

Physicians also suggest that they are being forced to practise costly "defensive medicine" through the increased use of diagnostic tests because of an increase in the number of medical malpractice lawsuits (Canadian Medical Association 1984, 46). The threat of litigation forces the doctor to balance the precautionary measures suggested by medical liability rules against the cost of redundant or marginally useful procedures (Economic Council of Canada 1987b, 160).

This fee-for-service model means that, even if provinces refuse to increase the fee scale, doctors can maintain their income by ordering more work for themselves or by sharing the same patient more widely (Economic Council of Canada 1987b, 15). Europe has long been aware of this problem of provider-induced demand and unnecessary referrals, and in many countries patients are locked in to the primary physician first chosen. This factor is especially important, since the number of physicians is growing. Adopting the European approach could provide another means of controlling the rate of increase of health care costs.

These considerations lead us to the third determinant; namely, the number of physicians. While provinces have worked hard to control hospital budgets and physicians' fee schedules, there has been little control over the supply of new physicians.

Canadian medical schools are currently turning out new physicians at a rate which, combined with residual immigration, is raising the supply by 1.5-2 percent per capita per year. At the same time, demographic trends are having a comparatively trivial impact on physician use, about 0.3 percent per capita per year (Canadian Medical Association 1984, 175).

This has put increased pressure on the doctors' access to the "free" capital and personnel provided by society through the hospital. "It is not, therefore, surprising that physicians perceive 'underfunding,' which places pressure on their productivity and earning ability at any given fee schedule" (Evans 1987, 174). Hence, instead of the aging population forcing society to increase the supply of physicians, the excess supply of physicians has applied new procedures and technologies to the elderly and increased the physician utilization rates among the elderly to satisfy their need for work and income (Evans 1987, 176).

An increased supply of physicians has the ability to increase health care costs more dramatically than the aging of the population.

A 10 percent increase in the numbers of the very elderly might lead to increased need of approximately 6,952 hospital days...

If physician supply in Manitoba were to increase 10 percent and physicians were to continue to hospitalize patients at approximately the same rate as they did prior to this increase (two very plausible assumptions), there would be an increased "need" for 113,888 hospital days (Economic Council of Canada 1987b, 56).

Obviously, there exists a range of problems, but policy alternatives have been suggested and will now be reviewed.

One alternative would be for Canada to return to a privately funded health care system. However, the pattern of health care costs in Canada versus the United States (see Figure 7.1) presents a convincing argument against privatization. If we had followed the U.S. model of private funding, there is no reason why our cost patterns would not have continued to mirror their trends. If so, we would now be spending about 25 percent more on health care, an increase of more than $10 billion (Evans 1987, 169). In defending a government-controlled system, health economist Robert Evans argues that the government can bargain more with physicians and others than any individual or a number of insurance agencies, and that this is the reason for Canada's success in controlling costs relative to the United States.

In terms of partial privatization, as in Britain (*e.g.*, user fees, coinsurance schemes), this would transfer part of the cost from the tax-paid system to the private sector to be paid either directly by the individual or by premiums for private health insurance, but would not necessarily reduce total health care costs. The idea that deterrent charges work assumes that users indulge in unnecessary services, or that one can tell what is necessary or unnecessary. There in no empirical proof of this (Economic Council of Canada 1987b, 158). What user fees may do is deter lower income users from early use of the system. Hence, a return to a privately funded system seems ill advised.

Several other methods of controlling health care costs, even with an aging population, are worthy of consideration. The most common method proposed is to decrease the rate of institutionalization of our elderly. As previously stated, not only do we institutionalize a disproportionate proportion of our elderly, but we often place them in inappropriate and inefficient settings. Although several provinces cover long term care under their health programs (there is no financial penalty for staying in a hospital bed), in practice, it is also difficult to move the elderly from one environment to another.

> First, there is often a problem with coordination of the various institutions, compounded by their division between the health and social services juris-diction. Second, there are so few vacant places available, that movement is virtually impossible. Thus, the patient who has entered hospital cannot be moved out again to a nursing home because his place has been filled. There perhaps would be vacant places in the nursing home if current residents who would be better in homes for the aged could find a spare place. Those in homes for the aged might be better in purpose-built apartments with supervision, and some occupying these apartments would be better in the community (Canadian Medical Association 1984, 30).

Demographic projections done by a Canadian Medical Association Task Force found that the 1.4 percent per annum growth in health care costs associated with the aging population and the present delivery system (see Section 7.5), could be reduced to 0.8 percent per annum principally by reduced institutionalization of the elderly (Canadian Medical Association 1984, 115). The more optimal placement of the elderly was identified as the largest potential source of savings in the cost of health care.

Hence, we need to redesign the delivery system so that the elderly are placed in the most efficient and appropriate setting. It is believed that from one-third to one-half of elderly Canadians who are presently in long-term care institutions would probably be able to live in the community, if support services were available (see Marshall 1987, 499; and Gross and Schwenger 1981, 83). This can be done with significant savings to the health care system.

> Canadian experience too shows that a package of home care services can be provided to elderly people within their own home for the "relatively controllable" cost of about 10 percent of the nursing home budget (Kane and Kane, 1985) with the additional prospect of restricting the growth of institutions (Economic Council of Canada 1987b, 37).
>
> Where disabilities become more severe, it is sometimes still possible for the family to provide the necessary support system, provided it is offered a little help. In this context, the Nova Scotian policy of offering relatives up to $4,800 per annum to care for elderly individuals who would otherwise be institutionalized and the Manitoba policy of allowing nursing homes to admit residents for very short stays in order to give their families periodic relief have much to recommend them (Pifer and Bronte 1986, 84).

At the moment, the elderly requiring long term care often find that the majority of their costs are covered in high-cost institutions such as hospitals but not in lower cost facilities such as nursing homes. This provides an incentive for the elderly and their families to utilize such high-cost facilities, often prior to actual necessity (International Social Security Association 1984, 94).

As of the early 1980s only three provinces (British Columbia, Manitoba, and Saskatchewan) had coordinated home care and community support programs; but as part of a general fiscal restraint program, B.C. has threatened severe monetary cutbacks to its program of coordination. Other provinces offer some of these services but only on an ad hoc basis (Chappell *et al.* 1986, 98).

Not only do costs rise if we inappropriately place the elderly who are capable of independent living in institutions, but we may also decrease the residents' quality of life. This has been referred to as the "warehousing" of the elderly (Canadian Medical Association 1984, 37). Thus we need more incentives to place elderly patients optimally among the service providers.

Other suggestions have also been made to enhance the cost effectiveness of the present health care delivery system. For example, concern has been expressed about costs associated with the use of new technologies, especially those that prolong life but provide no "cure," referred to as "halfway technologies." Few of these technologies have had a dramatic effect on health status (Economic Council of Canada 1987b, 116), and many of them have to be used continually by the patient which is often very expensive (Economic Council of Canada 1987b, 118). Examples include organ transplants, the computed tomography (CT) scanner, and artificial limbs and organs.

There is often no central agency which manages the allocation of resources. Adjacent hospitals may request and receive similar technologies if they have sufficient political skill, while entire regions do without (Economic Council of Canada 1987b, 135). For example, two of Ontario's three magnetic resonance imaging (MRI) machines are located in hospitals in London (Economic Council of Canada 1987b, 135).

Further, new technologies are often in place prior to proper evaluation. They may then be used with too high a frequency in situations where their use is not cost effective, because an equally good, lower cost technology is available, or where the use of the new technology places the patient at increased risk (Canadian Medical Association 1984, 52). At the same time, the use of "low ticket, high volume" procedures should continue to be monitored to be sure that they are not used inappropriately (*e.g.*, in defensive medicine as a result of concern over medical litigation). Because new technologies can and do prolong life, their non-use raises special moral and practical issues that will be difficult to resolve (Canadian Medical Association 1984, xi). Who will receive the kidney transplant or the artificial heart? Who will decide and how?

A change in the accounting system used for the delivery of health care has also been suggested. Presently, most governments reimburse health care providers on a cost-reimbursement system. Whenever a bill is submitted, it is paid. Hospitals are reimbursed on the basis of global budgets, which are fixed operating budgets set annually for each hospital. This approach provides little incentive for hospitals to provide their services efficiently, especially if operating deficits are routinely covered. This is now an issue in the province of Ontario.

One alternative that has been proposed is a new payment and accounting system based on diagnosis related groups (DRGS) (Economic Council of Canada 1987b, 184). Under this method, if a particular procedure has a certain average cost, then the hospital would be paid that average amount. If actual costs are less, the hospital keeps the difference; if more, they are responsible for the loss. If, over time, this method leads to overall lower costs, they would be reflected in future average payments, leading to cost savings for the taxpayer. Hospitals are thus provided with a financial incentive to lower average costs, something that is not available today.

Similarly, the cost-based reimbursement system for physicians has also been criticized for not providing financial incentives for lower cost treatment techniques. A model used successfully in the U.S. of pre-paid practice arrangements has been suggested as an alternative. Under this system, doctors are paid a set amount per patient per year (*i.e.*, per capita, which leads to the name "capitation" payment or "capitated" medical practice). There is no incentive for the doctor to make use of unnecessary services under this system. Regardless of the work done, the payment to the doctor is set, in advance, on a per capita basis. This fee, however, may vary according to the age of the patient.

Experience from the U.S. indicates that changing from the fee-for-service model to the capitated-medical-practice model can lead to reductions in hospital usage of 20 to 40 percent with no apparent harm to patients (Canadian Medical Association 1984, 173). A similar experiment at Algoma Steel in Sault Ste. Marie, Ontario, resulted in lower hospital and surgical rates; for example, rates for tonsillectomy and adenoidectomy were one-third of their previous levels (Pifer and Bronte 1986, 87).

It is believed that the alternatives outlined above could result in significant cost savings by providing proper incentives for those who control the health care delivery system; namely, the hospitals and the physicians.

Another suggestion is for better coordination between long term care and short term care providers. As previously noted in this section, these two subsystems are managed separately and independently at present (often under two government ministries), causing duplication and inefficiency (Economic Council of Canada 1987a). For example, in the province of Ontario, homes for the aged are part of the Ministry of Community and Social Services. However, once patients require at least one-and-a-half hours of supervised extended care per day, they come under *The Nursing Homes Act* and become the responsibility of the Minister of Health.

Researchers also complain about the difficulty in obtaining data beyond those for acute care hospitals and physicians. Long term care utilization data (including home care) and data on housing are either non-existent, incomplete, or inaccurate (Marshall 1987, 516), making it difficult for researchers to analyse policy alternatives and present clear arguments for systems that may be more cost effective. Also, data on hospitals and physicians may not be available in a form that allows analysis broken down by age, beyond age 65 (*i.e.*, 65-74, 75-84, 85+) (Marshall 1987, 516).

Finally, little is done to measure the effectiveness of the dollars we spend. For example, Canada does not conduct national health surveys, as does the United States (Marshall 1987, 500). Thus, we have no way of knowing if our tax dollars are being spent effectively in the health care field. At the least, it is suggested that costs of particular health services (and, if possible the alternatives) should be publicized to consumers and providers. The media should be encouraged to quote costs (Canadian Medical Association 1984, 114). The education of the consumer to the alternatives will allow for cost control efforts at the level of the individual service user.

Canada is now in the position where so much money is being spent on hospital care and the associated new technologies that the alternative service providers, which may be more efficient, are being neglected (Marshall 1987, 512).
A shift from providing the "best possible care regardless of cost" will not be easy, however. While we, as a society, may deem a service or technology to be uneconomic, the individual with the disease may not be impressed with our assessment and will press for its implementation. "The fact that uneconomic health care services may be demanded by fully informed and perfectly rational patients indicates the ultimate economic problem associated with the health care sector" (Pifer and Bronte 1986, 49).

An analogy from a recent Health Care Colloquium notes:

We can decide that installing warning beacons in private airplanes... is not cost-effective. When an identifiable small aircraft crashes in deep bush, we willingly spend far more in the search and rescue efforts... As those who might be saved by an intervention can be identified and named, it becomes remarkably hard to refuse on the national grounds of insufficient cost-effectiveness (Economic Council of Canada 1987b, 135).

In the same way, it is relatively easy to advocate a reduction in the use of high cost technologies especially for patients who are clearly terminal. However, while that may be logical on a macro economic basis, it may prove difficult to implement once the individual being affected is identifiable.

7.7 CONCLUSIONS

This chapter reviewed the present health care delivery system and noted general agreement that the present delivery model is inefficient and may lead to inappropriate care for the elderly. It was noted that this delivery system is very expensive and, without revision, can be expected to become more costly as the population ages. Moreover, we expect that health care costs will rise more rapidly than inflation. There is an anticipated 1 percent per annum excess growth because of inefficiencies in the provider system and 1.4 percent per annum excess growth due to population aging (Canadian Medical Association 1984, 115). If inefficiencies in the current delivery system are not addressed, governments will face funding constraints. "They are trapped by a combination of slow economic growth and taxpayer resistance into mounting deficits and the need to cut public expenditures. They will have great difficulty meeting current spending commitments, let alone coping with the increases in costs which will come with the aging population" (Evans 1987, 166).

As stated in Chapter 1, the perception of funding problems can create feelings of economic insecurity as surely as would a true funding crisis. Hence, not only must we strive to control the rise in health care costs, that ability must also be communicated to the users of the system. Canadians must be assured that rising health care costs will not pose a threat to the total social security system as it now exists. Otherwise, economic insecurity will be the result. Chapter 8 analyses similar funding issues as they pertain to our retirement income security system.

CHAPTER 8

FUTURE FUNDING OF SOCIAL SECURITY

8.1 INTRODUCTION

Previous references to a poll (Allenvest Group Limited) suggested that Canadians are more concerned about the security of their government-funded social security benefits (*e.g.*, OAS, GIS, C/QPP) than about their employer-sponsored or individually funded schemes (see Sections 4.9 and 6.5). We also noted in the conclusions to Chapters 4 through 6 some reasons for this sense of insecurity. This chapter attempts to analyse these concerns to see if they are real or merely inaccurate perceptions; it also analyses possible funding alternatives for social security.

There are two basic methods of funding retirement-income security schemes. Under the pay-as-you go method used by almost all government-sponsored schemes worldwide, benefits are paid out of current contributions, and little or no assets accumulate. If contributions cease, benefits also cease, almost immediately. The continued payment of benefits is contingent upon the continued willingness of workers to contribute, or pay taxes.

Employer-sponsored plans and individual schemes, on the other hand, are fully funded, with each participant having real assets backing the promised benefit. Such plans are insecure only to the extent that certain funding assumptions turn out to be incorrect; for example, the assumed rate of investment return may not be realized. Thus, these plans are immune to the effects of population aging (see also Chapter 2).

Government-sponsored plans, however, are affected by changing demographics since the level of contributions (or taxes) required is a function of the ratio of the number of beneficiaries to the number of contributors.

One other attribute of pay-as-you-go plans has an impact on public policy. In the early stages of most pay-as-you-go systems, contributions tend to exceed benefits, because the initial population of contributors normally exceeds the initial group of beneficiaries, and the original group of beneficiaries, having made no contributions, are granted benefits which are usually smaller or delayed relative to what will be paid once the scheme matures. Hence, there is a natural tendency for the costs of pay-as-you-go schemes to rise as the schemes mature, and then to level off when the plan is "fully mature" (see Keyfitz 1984a).

If a pay-as-you-go scheme is maturing at the same time as the underlying population is aging, then these two shifts will have a cumulative effect on the costs of the plan. That is the case in Canada. The analysis presented will show that the costs of funding our social security systems over the next half-century will rise (this appears to be true under a wide variety of possible demographic assumptions) and more rapidly than the costs associated with health care (see Section 7.5).

While the analysis shows an expectation of rapidly rising costs, the problem remains of turning these concerns into public policy action. The cost increases presented will not become a serious problem until the next century, and politicians, historically, have focussed on concerns that have an impact prior to the next election. This tends to result in many long-term demographic problems ultimately becoming "inevitable surprises" (see Keyfitz 1984a, 2; and Foot 1982, 123). Also, the key economic and demographic assumptions upon which many of these schemes were originally designed (*i.e.*, mid 1960s) no longer hold true.

> People were not at all conscious of it in those distant early days, but their confidence in social security rested on growth — of population, income and scope of the schemes - and with the threatened cessation of growth social insurance schemes will become much more expensive; the foreshadowing of this is part of what is responsible for the present demoralization (Keyfitz 1984a, 3).

8.2 SOCIAL SECURITY FUNDING UNDER POPULATION AGING

Myers summarizes the connection between our aging population and why it will affect the funding of our pay-as-you-go social security system as follows:

> If all other demographic elements are constant, higher fertility rates will have a favourable effect on social insurance systems providing old-age retirement benefits. As long as fertility is above the replacement rate (or the actual fertility plus the effect of net immigration achieves this result), there will be a steadily growing covered work force to provide the contributions necessary to support the retired population. This type of chain-letter effect will show relatively low costs for the social insurance program, although eventually the chain must break (because population size cannot increase forever), and the cost of the program will become significantly higher (Myers 1985a, 3).

Commentators on problems of population aging often analyse the effect of one particular variable by holding all other demographic elements constant. This deterministic approach has been criticized by many social demographers (*e.g.*, see McDaniel 1986, Chapter 2) since, in the real world, any change in one factor will affect the entire demographic structure, so that a one-parameter-at-a-time approach may be inappropriate.

The commentary that follows might be viewed as such a deterministic, parameter-specific analysis. In its defence, however, it should be noted that the magnitude of the demographic shift that will take place during the next half-century in Canada is such that virtually any "believable" set of demographic assumptions will lead to results very similar to those presented below. For example:

> Denton and Spencer explored other possible sets of assumptions, but with the possible exception of the "high" fertility projection (in which the total fertility rate is assumed to rise in equal annual increments from 1.7 births per women to 3.0 by 1996, remaining at that level thereafter), the general population and labour force patterns are broadly similar to those described for the medium assumptions projections (Seward 1987, 14).

That is, the results presented in this chapter are broadly accepted by various authors (*e.g.*, see Fellegi 1988).

Section 2.2 noted how the age structure of the Canadian population will change in the next forty years, from being a very "young" population to being a relatively "old" population. This chapter will investigate its impact on the funding of social security.

The basic social security benefits, OAS + GIS / SPA, are funded by general tax revenues. The source of general tax revenues is the productive capacity of the labour force. Table 8.1 presents data that provide a starting point for analysis.

TABLE 8.1
LABOUR FORCE DEPENDENCY RATIOS

Year	Population (,000)	Labour Force LF (,000)	Pop. 0-19/ LF	Pop. 65+/ LF	Total* Ratio
	(1)	(2)	(3)	(4)	(5)
1986	25591	12898	0.57	0.21	0.78
1991	26783	13767	0.54	0.23	0.77
1996	27766	14494	0.51	0.25	0.75
2001	28524	15090	0.48	0.25	0.74
2006	29131	15364	0.46	0.27	0.72
2011	29648	15418	0.44	0.30	0.73
2016	30063	15163	0.43	0.35	0.78
2021	30318	14770	0.44	0.41	0.85
2026	30367	14408	0.44	0.47	0.92
2031	30219	14083	0.44	0.52	0.97
2036	29909	13862	0.44	0.54	0.98

*Column (5) may not equal (3) + (4) because of rounding
SOURCE: Denton and Spencer 1987, Tables 2, 3, 6 Standard Assumptions.

Given that the labour force is the source of production that results in taxable revenues, and that the population aged 65 and over represents the beneficiaries of the government social security system, then it can be seen that the "aged dependency ratio" (column 4) will more than double in the next fifty years (157 percent growth). Chapter 2 explained that while this increase is partly a result of the enhanced life expectancy of individual Canadians, it is far more the result of the decline in fertility rates. However, while expenditures for the aged dependents will rise, because of the decline in fertility rates, expenditures for the youth dependents are expected to fall (see Fellegi 1988). Hence, the total dependency ratio (youth plus aged as presented in column (5)) does not rise nearly as rapidly as the aged dependency ratio (25 percent versus 157 percent growth by 2036).

As a result, some observers (*e.g.*, McDaniel 1986) conclude that all that may be required is a shift in resources from the youth dependents to the elderly sector. The 25 percent growth in the total dependency ratio over the next 50 years should be less than the expected expansion in the economy (25 percent growth over 50 years only requires a GNP growth of 0.45 percent per annum), and would thus be readily affordable.

Others, however, have pointed out problems with this analysis (*e.g.*, Foot 1982, 134-43). McDaniel's conclusion assumes both that government expenditures on the young are the same per capita as those on the elderly, and that resources can be transferred readily from the young to the old. Foot estimates that government expenditures on the elderly are roughly two-and-a-half times greater per capita than those on the young. Hence, a rise in the number of elderly, even if it were completely offset by a decrease in the number of youths (which it is not), would not result in constant government expenditures. As to transferability, there would be significant costs associated with the relocation of resources (*e.g.*, retraining of workers). Further, different levels of government are responsible for different types of public expenditures. Hence, the relocation of resources may demand a renegotiation of federal-provincial cost-sharing agreements, which is by no means an easy task.

Returning to Table 8.1 and accepting that Foot is correct in assuming a 2.5 to 1 cost deferential per capita for the elderly versus the young, Table 8.1 can be revised and presented in a more meaningful way. Table 8.2, column (1), is simply the Total Dependency Ratio of Table 8.1 column (5) presented relative to the base year, 1986 (*i.e.*, 1986 equals 1.00). Column (2) of Table 8.2 is calculated by applying a weight of one to the young dependents and a weight of 2.5 to the aged dependents. The column labelled "Expenditures Dependency Ratio" is the resulting total relative to the base year, 1986. That is, column (2) of Table 8.2 represents the expected growth in government expenditures per unit of labour compared with the base year 1986 (again 1986 equals 1.00).

TABLE 8.2

DEPENDENCY RATIO GROWTH PATTERN

Year	Total Dependency Ratio Growth Pattern	Expenditures Dependency Ratio Growth Pattern
	(1)	(2)
1986	1.00	1.00
1991	0.98	1.01
1996	0.96	1.02
2001	0.94	1.02
2006	0.92	1.02
2011	0.93	1.07
2016	1.00	1.19
2021	1.08	1.33
2026	1.17	1.47
2031	1.24	1.60
2036	1.25	1.63

Work by Foot indicates that, depending on the demographic assumptions, the 63 percent growth by 2036 represents the peak of total government expenditures on aged plus young dependents. (See also Fellegi 1988).

What is the reason for this 63 percent rise in those government expenditures during the next half-century? Part of this increase can be explained by the rise in health care costs that would be generated by a "status quo" model (*i.e.*, no change in the present level or method of health care delivery). Denton and Spencer (1984b, 14) state that health care costs will rise 69.8 percent during the fifty-year period (see Section 7.5). They note that the use of alternate demographic assumptions changes the rate of increase, but in every case the rise in health costs is large and is the second most important single factor.

The most important factor in rising government expenditures, however, is the provision of social security (*e.g.*, OAS and GIS). Again quoting Denton and Spencer:

> The greatest of the population-induced increases by far is in the category of social security. The inevitable rise in the number of older people causes an increase of almost 30 percent in social security costs between 1980 and 1990 and of more than 50 percent by the year 2000. By the year 2030, social security costs are roughly three times their 1980 level. These results are virtually the same whichever of the seven population projections is considered. Under present institutional arrangements, the costs of social security in Canada are going to rise very sharply in this decade and the ones to follow (Denton and Spencer 1984b, 14). (See also Marshall 1987, 576, and Fellegi 1988).

However, government expenditures for the young (for example, education costs) are expected to fall. In most other categories of expenditures, there will be some increases in costs, but these will be minor (less than the rate of growth of the population) (Denton and Spencer 1984b, 20). In total, these models predict a 63 percent rise in government expenditures in the next 50 years because of population aging, with the primary cause being the funding requirements of the social security system.

Private pension plans, because they are fully funded, are not affected by these shifting demographics. The C/QPP is affected, but not necessarily in the same manner as the tax-revenue funded OAS and GIS.

In Section 4.6, we outlined the funding history of the C/QPP and noted that contribution rates were already formulated to rise. From 1966 to 1986, the combined employer-employee C/QPP contribution rate was set at 3.6 percent of earnings up to the Year's Maximum Pensionable Earnings (YMPE) minus the Year's Basic Exemption (YBE) which is 10 percent of the YMPE. Starting in 1987, contribution rates started to rise and will reach 7.60 percent by 2011 according to the agreed schedule. Even with this agreed-to rise in the contribution rate, expenditures from the CPP fund are projected to exceed total income (contributions plus investment earnings) in 1999. Further, the projected ultimate contribution rate is estimated to exceed 13 percent of earnings up to the Average Industrial Wage, or more than three times the 1989 contribution rate (Canada, Office of the Superintendent of Financial Institutions 1988, 16). This is on the assumption that benefits are not increased from today's levels (see also Asimakopulos 1984).

This required increase in C/QPP contribution rates is mainly because of the effects of population aging, but also partly because of the maturation of the plan, as explained in Section 8.1. As these necessary contribution increases have become more widely known, pressure to expand the benefits of the C/QPP has declined. As the 1984 Ontario Proposals for Pension Reform state:

> While the principles governing the CPP's benefit structure are well established, the principles that govern the Plan's long-run financing remain ambiguous... Perhaps its most serious deficiency is that the Plan's contribution rate gives an unrealistically low measure of the true cost of benefits promised (Treasurer of Ontario 1984, 37).

Canadians have no individual contractual guarantee that their C/QPP benefits will be paid. Instead there exists a statutory contract with the next generation. The aging population, however, means that while the present generation of contributors has had approximately six contributors per beneficiary, the next generation will only have three. The question remains (see Allenvest Group Limited 1985) whether the next generation of workers (taxpayers) and contributors will deem these benefits to be affordable. If they do not, then the next generation of social security beneficiaries will not receive the benefits they are now being promised. Any doubts about the willingness of future generations to fund these rising social security costs would inevitably result in individual perceptions of economic insecurity. Recent tax-back amendments to OAS only reinforce this sense of insecurity.

8.3 PUBLIC POLICY ALTERNATIVES FOR THE FUNDING OF SOCIAL SECURITY

It was shown in Section 7.5 that health care costs would rise about 70 percent over the next half-century. However, research cited states that this will be affordable within a growing economy, especially if public policy can focus on inefficiencies within the system. At the same time, we are faced with social security costs that are projected to triple during the same period of time. Since the social security delivery system is efficient, no savings can be expected because of a change in the delivery model. The question remains as to whether future generations will be willing to fund these rising costs.

In the United States, where the funding of the social security system is based on contributions from earnings and not general tax revenues, significant increases in the contribution rate have been accepted without noticeable protest (see Myers 1985b, 29). One reason for this acceptance is that people apparently prefer a strong social security system to the alternative of returning the financial responsibility for the elderly to the family (Pifer and Bronte 1986, 43). On the other hand, in countries like Italy, where most of the funding for social security comes from general tax revenues, taxpayers have reacted to increased costs for social security either by drawing more earnings from the "underground" economy (*i.e.*, untaxed income) or by striving to maintain lower levels of benefits (Pifer and Bronte 1986, 255).

What follows is an analysis of the public policy alternatives to overcome problems in the funding of social security benefits.

Fertility

As noted earlier in this chapter, higher fertility rates have a favourable effect on social insurance systems. If the working population grows, individual contribution levels can be relatively low, but as the proportion of the population that is elderly increases, so too must contribution rates.

At present, the Canadian fertility rate is around 1.67, whereas a fertility rate of 2.10 is required just to maintain our present population, assuming zero net migration. Although it would take a large rise in fertility rates to stabilize social security costs, any rise in fertility rates would help to ease the funding problem.

Two basic schools of thought exist as to the future level of fertility rates. One school is represented by the Easterlin "wave-theory" of fertility (Easterlin 1987). Easterlin postulates that fertility rates rise and fall in a wave-like pattern with a cycle length (peak-to-peak or trough-to-trough) of two generations. Easterlin says that a small cohort (like that born in the

1930s) will find life easier than expected. Jobs are plentiful, advancement is fast, wealth is accumulated more easily than anticipated. Such a cohort will tend to have large families (as they did).

On the other hand, a large cohort (for example, those born in the 1950s and early 1960s) will find life more difficult than expected. Unemployment is high, prices are inflated, advancement is slow, and wealth is more difficult to accumulate. Such a cohort will tend to have smaller families. If Easterlin is correct, there should now exist indications of a turn-around in the fertility rates (which, in fact, has not happened).

The other common theory on fertility is presented by Ermisch (1983), Butz and Ward (1979), and others. The theory states that in a one-earner family, if the worker's real wages rise rapidly and the cost of children remains constant, that family will have more children, which is what happened in the 1950s and 1960s. In a two-earner family, however, if real wages rise rapidly, but the wife has to leave the workforce, or interrupt a career path, to have and raise children, then the "cost" of children rises and fertility rates will not change. Ermisch presents data that show that the higher a woman's earning power, the larger the gap between marriage and first birth. He also points out that the increased probability of divorce may keep the fertility rate down, since children complicate divorce. Therefore, this school of thought sees no reason to believe that fertility rates will rise at all. It anticipates that they will level off at about their present level, which is well below a replacement rate.

The province of Quebec has recently passed legislation in an attempt to increase the number of births. Quebec has the lowest fertility rate in Canada, at 1.38. The only jurisdiction with a lower rate is West Germany. Quebec will pay families $500 cash for their first baby, $1,000 for their second, and $4,500 each for the third and subsequent children. A new monthly allowance for children under six, ranging from $8 to $41, will be added to current provincial family allowance payments. Also, these payments will no longer be taxable.

Evidence from other countries suggests that these incentives have little effect (Hohn 1987, 461). For example, West Germany offered cash incentives for women to have children, extended mothers' holidays and child-care facilities, but the fertility rate continued to slide. In fact, the countries that have the largest family allowances also have the lowest birth rates (Weitz 1979, 21).

Finally, raising fertility rates could create its own problems, since it would result in increased youth dependents (McDaniel 1987, 334). This would only exacerbate the total dependency burden as presented in Table 8.1.

Immigration

Increased net immigration has a similar effect on dependency ratios as increased fertility, and may even be superior if workers enter after being educated and prepared for the workforce. However, the Economic Council of Canada study *One in Three* points out that increased immigration today is not desirable, since most of these immigrants would be the same age as the Baby Boom cohort, thus exacerbating the ratio problem. In fact, increased immigration is not desirable until the decade prior to 2031.

> We noted earlier that the retirement income programs would reach just over 7 percent of GNP by 2031, assuming moderate population growth and maintenance of the present age of eligibility and income-replacement ratio. To reduce this share by only 1 percentage point would necessitate an additional 2.8 million workers in the labour force and no extra retirees by 2031. To accomplish this would require... an increase in net immigration in the decade prior to 2031 from 80,000 to 640,000, assuming, as is now the case, that only half of the immigrants would be of workforce age.

There are two other factors which should be considered. First, while historically immigrants came to Canada from Europe, Europe is suffering from its own decline in birth rates and may, therefore, not be able to supply us with future workers. Instead, we must expect that the majority of new immigrants will be "visible minorities," which may necessitate special social service programs to enhance assimilation.

Second, our present immigration criteria set very high standards for potential immigrants. This means that, for many developing nations, countries like Canada take many of their best individuals, which results in a retardation of their own rates of economic improvement.

Economic Growth

A tripling of social security costs during the next fifty years appears formidable, but is equivalent to only a 2.2 percent per annum growth. That is, if we can achieve a 2.2 percent per annum growth in the Gross National Product during the next fifty years, then social security costs will consume no more of tax revenues than they do today. Many researchers believe that this rate of economic growth is achievable. During the period 1927 to 1983, economic growth was 2.2 percent per annum. However, during the decade ending in 1983, economic growth was close to zero (Denton and Spencer 1984a, 19); hence, some view the required 2.2 percent growth assumption as optimistic.

Economic growth is dependent upon three input variables; namely, labour, capital, and the state of technology (see Denton and Spencer 1987, 17). As the Baby Boom begins to retire after 2011 and is followed in the labour force by the Baby Bust, the number of labour units will decline. Hence, without extraordinary immigration, or a sharp rise in labour force participation rates, economic growth will not be the result of labour force growth (see Foot 1982, 212).

Denton and Spencer (1987) submit, therefore, that future production capacity depends on how technological advances are introduced. They differentiate between "embodied technological change" that can only be introduced to newly produced machines and workers. Once introduced, the new technology is "fixed" for the life of the machine or worker so that the rate at which new technology can affect production capacity is limited to the rate at which new cohorts are added to the stock of capital or labour.

"Disembodied technological change," however, is seen to affect the production characteristics of all existing units in equal proportion, whether they are newly trained or experienced workers. If technological advances are "disembodied" they have more chance to affect the economy's productive capacity, at least in the short run.

In general, labour force productivity levels rise as workers age, quickly at first, and then more gradually. Hence the ability for enhanced productivity of those in the Baby Boom cohort may act as a counterbalance to the slower anticipated growth in the labour force in total. Further, to the extent that younger workers are better trained or educated, there will be a further rise in productivity levels as the younger workers take the place of older ones (Denton and Spencer 1987, 20).

There are other related issues. First, the 2.2 percent growth rate in social security costs assumes no enhancement in benefits for fifty years. If the standard of living of the active work force improves at a rate of 2.2 percent per annum, the elderly may face a half-century of benefit levels that do not increase at all except to cover the rate of inflation. Any real improvements in benefits, over and above the rate of inflation will mean an expansion of social security as a proportion of GNP.

Second, as long as social security consumes its present percentage of tax revenues (which requires 2.2 percent annual real growth in GNP), there will be no room to expand other social security programs, such as enhanced day care benefits, or worker retraining programs, without increasing the overall tax rate. Thus, new government benefits may have to be postponed or curtailed.

In fact, even at today's rate of expenditure, government expenditures exceed tax revenues to a significant extent. For example, the federal government is currently operating at an annual deficit of around $30 billion, and the total federal debt is now over $320 billion, or about $12,500 per capita. Out of every tax dollar about 30 percent is required to service this debt. The national debt used to be around 25 percent of GNP, and it is now close to 60 percent (Task Force on Inflation Protection, Vol. 1 1988, 15). Presently the government is looking for ways to decrease the size of the national deficit and is more likely to be searching for ways to constrain costs rather than expanding programs. Thus, we see that:

> The growing size of budget deficits has narrowed the federal government's room to manoeuvre. Unless contained they would reach a critical mass at

which the cost of servicing more debt will lead to even greater deficits. At present, therefore, there is not much capacity to expand on existing programs and little or no capacity to embark on major new expenditure programs (Economics Council of Canada 1987b, 194).

Age of Eligibility

The labour force participation rates of men aged 55-64 have been falling. For women it has remained relatively level for the past decade, while the participation rates in all other ages have risen (McDonald, Warner 1990, 41). This drop in work activity for the age group 55-64 has been accelerated by government and employer programs which encourage older workers to retire early (*e.g.*, flexible retirement age under the C/QPP). These programs were adopted largely because of the relatively high levels of unemployment in the young labour force in that if an older worker retires, it may create an opening for a younger unemployed worker. However, the Baby Boom is now largely in the labour force. Following it is the Baby Bust cohort. In the future there may be pressure toward keeping older workers in the labour force for longer periods of time, for two reasons. First, they will be needed as workers because of a decline in the supply of labour, and second, the cost of their retirement income may create pressure to delay paying retirement benefits until higher ages (Marshall 1987, 157, 193; and Pifer and Bronte 1986, 374, 388).

There are also sociological reasons for raising the age of eligibility for retirement income benefits, since it seems both illogical and unfair to relegate the experience and expertise of capable older workers to empty role structures merely because they attain a certain chronological age (Marshall 1987, 196; and Pifer and Bronte 1986, 65).

> Legal pensionable age bears no direct relation to an individual's health; at least not in the sense that the former is based on the latter. It is worth reminding ourselves of this to appreciate that a particular chronological age for retirement is based on social conventions and not on any physiological phenomenon... As things stand, "the old" are considered "inactive" and often they become indeed inactive not only in the economic sense. Here we have therefore a kind of self-fulfilling prophecy (Rhee 1974, 17).

This same author points out that, ironically, geriatric hospitals often use "makework" projects as a health restoring activity (ergo therapy) (Rhee 1974, 222). For these workers, the ability to stay in the workforce would lead to an enhanced health profile. Forcing workers between ages 55 to 65 to retire to create jobs for younger workers may only replace one inactive group by another. What is needed is a way to decrease the ratio of inactive, to active, workers.

The myth that age results in declining productivity has proven difficult to modify (Pifer and Bronte 1986, 348). However, as McPherson (1983, 376) observes:

1. There is relatively little decline in productivity with age.
2. There is some loss of muscular strength and endurance.
3. Reaction time slows with age but experience at the task may offset the losses.
4. There is little decline in intelligence affecting job performance.
5. Older workers are generally more satisfied with their jobs and are less likely to leave an organization for another job (perhaps because they have few alternatives).
6. Decremental changes in job-related aptitudes or skills do not occur at the same rate (for example, a hearing loss may not be accompanied by a slow reaction time or by a loss of visual activity), and those that do occur may be compensated for by experience.
7. Declining cognitive or physical skills can be overcome by a willingness to resort to coping strategies (such as a reliance on co-workers for assistance, taking work home).
8. Older workers are absent less often and have fewer accidents than younger workers.

In general, research shows that for most workers and occupations, productivity does not peak until after age 50, and often not until age 60, and then the decline in productivity is slow (Pifer and Bronte 1986, 371).

Another reason for looking at an increase in the age of eligibility for social security benefits is demographic. If life expectancy continues to increase at its present rate, the period for which benefits are paid will rise significantly. In the United States, Myers looked at a model for age of eligibility that kept constant the ratio of retirement life expectancy to working life expectancy (between age 20 and the retirement age). Under this model, the following are equivalent ages at retirement.

TABLE 8.3

EQUIVALENT AGE AT RETIREMENT (U.S.)

1940	65 years
1985	69 years, 2 months
2000	70 years, 7 months
2060	73 years, 1 month

Source: Chen 1987, 411.

When the C/QPP and GIS were introduced in Canada in 1966, the age for full benefit entitlement was set at 65. Given the improvement in mortality from 1966 to 1986 and assuming consistent percentage improvement in the future, the following are equivalent ages at retirement (author's calculations):

TABLE 8.4
EQUIVALENT AGE AT RETIREMENT (CANADA)

Year	Age
1966	65.00
1981	67.30
1991	68.36
2001	69.36
2011	69.86
2021	70.28
2031	70.72

Brown and Iglesias (1989) performed detailed research to determine the age of eligibility that could be set so as to achieve constant expenditure dependency ratios (defined in Section 8.2; see Table 8.2) in the next century. The authors found that the expenditure dependency ratio remained relatively level from the year 2000 until 2006. It was at this point that they developed a shift in the age of eligibility for government-sponsored benefits that would work to keep the expenditure dependency ratio level. The result was an age of eligibility that rose from age 65 in 2006, by two months each year (starting in 2007) until it finally reached age 69 in 2030. No further adjustment was necessary.

This raising of the age of eligibility for government-sponsored retirement income does not imply that Canadians could not continue to retire whenever they wished. It merely means that the age of entitlement to federal income benefits would be extended to a slightly later age. Many Canadians retire before age 65 today, and this early retirement capability would not be affected.

This philosophy of controlling the rise in the costs of social security by raising the age of entitlement was incorporated into the social security system of the United States in the amendments of 1983. According to these amendments, the normal retirement age (the youngest age at which full unreduced benefits may be taken) will be raised gradually from age 65 in 2002 to age 66 by 2008 and then in gradual steps to age 67 in 2027.

By announcing this change in 1983, the Old Age Security Administration allowed the individual U.S. worker sufficient time to modify any retirement schemes already in place. For the same reason, any similar amendment in Canada should be made soon. This is especially true since workers in Canada now expect earlier, not later, retirement and because government policy today is to encourage early retirement. In this regard, it is noteworthy that the significant rise in the aged dependency ratio does not occur until after 2010. Although this may seem a long way off, those workers are now in the labour force and may now be designing their retirement savings schemes.

In summary, the elderly can continue to be treated as a dependent group. On the other hand, the promotion of continued participation of the elderly in the productive labour force will transform an increased aged dependency burden into an impetus for economic growth.

8.4 DISCLOSURE OF INFORMATION

Britain and the United States now regularly and publicly disclose long-term forecasts of their social security systems. The Parliamentary Task Force on Pension Reform (Canada 1983, 42) recommended that CPP contribution rates be scheduled for a 25-year period in advance. The province of Ontario (Treasurer of Ontario 1984, 40) proposed that any CPP benefits enrichment be tied to a formula that would require current CPP contribution rates to rise enough to pay the full cost of the additional benefits being promised. To allow for understanding of the full range of government-sponsored social security, this increased disclosure of information should not only include the C/QPP, but also the OAS/GIS system paid from general tax revenues.

8.5 A COMPARISON OF WESTERN SOCIAL SECURITY SYSTEMS

The definition of "social security" varies from country to country. In all countries social security includes government-sponsored retirement income security programs, but in several countries this is only the beginning. Some countries have a totally integrated social security system that includes health care, workers' compensation, and unemployment insurance. While Canada has all of these programs sponsored by the government, they do not all come to mind within the phrase social security, especially since most social security programs fall under provincial jurisdiction and therefore vary from province to province.

In the United States, the major components of the government-sponsored social security program are the Old-Age Survivors and Disability Insurance System (OASDI), the Hospital Insurance System (HI), and the Supplementary Medical Insurance System (SMI). For individuals under age 65, health care must be arranged through private resources (*e.g.*, personally purchased health care insurance). In most states, workers' compensation is also purchased through the private sector. This divergence of benefits covered by social security systems makes an international comparison of these systems difficult and, in some ways, meaningless.

Table 8.5 presents data on the contributions required from employers and employees for several major social security programs.

TABLE 8.5
COMPARATIVE CONTRIBUTIONS FOR MAJOR SOCIAL SECURITY PROGRAMS, 1981

Country	Combined Employee-Employer Contributions All Social Security Programs % of Earnings	Old-Age Invalids and Survivors Insurance % of Earnings
Austria	43.70	21.10
Belgium	37.87	15.11
Canada	8.44	3.60
France	47.55	13.00
West Germany	34.40	18.50
Italy	55.02	24.46
Japan	22.07	10.60
Netherlands	57.65	34.90
Sweden	35.20	21.15
Switzerland	17.72	9.40
United Kingdom	21.45	n.a.
United States	18.00	10.70

Sources: Alicia Munnell, "A Calm Look at Social Security." As quoted in Shultz, *The Economics of Aging*, 3rd edition, 1985.

The Canadian figures appear surprisingly low and cannot be explained solely by the fact that in 1981 Canada had one of the youngest populations of the countries listed. The key to the disparity is the source of funding. Table 8.5 only lists contributions that are an earmarked percentage of earnings. For example, the 3.60 percent contribution in Canada, under "Old-Age," represents the 1981 C/QPP contribution rate. Because OAS and GIS are paid for out of general tax revenues they are not included at all in this Table.

In terms of public pension plans only, there is still a wide variance in benefits and related costs.

The Federal Republic of Germany, France and Sweden have the most costly public pension programs (and the most costly social security programs), in part because the plan benefit is richer, in part because of the demographic structure of these countries. In 1983, expenditures for public pensions in the Federal Republic of Germany and France amounted to over 12 percent of the GDP of these countries, and to a little under 12 percent of GDP in Sweden... In contrast, the United Kingdom spent 7 percent of GDP on pensions in 1983, and the United States 8 percent. Canada spent 5 percent. One of the reasons the amount is as low as it is in the United Kingdom is that the public earnings-related plan was introduced in 1978, and will not mature until 1990. Public plans in Canada and the United States are paying out full benefits, but both countries have a more favourable demographic structure than the European countries (And this situation will change after the year 2010 when the "baby plans in all three countries are less generous than their European counterparts (Task Force on Inflation Protection, Vol. 2 1988, 256).

All of the systems reviewed are funded on a pay-as-you-go basis. Many of the European systems were once on a fully funded basis; however, the hyper-inflation experienced in many of the countries from 1929 to 1949 convinced them that the pay-as-you-go funding model would be more secure.

In this regard it should be noted that the two possible funding mechanisms entail different risks. Under the fully funded system, the retirees' benefits are contingent upon the real rate of return (i.e., after inflation) earned by the invested pension funds. In a pay-as-you-go system there are no (or small) investable funds, and retirees' benefits vary depending on labour productivity and the ratio of the number of beneficiaries to the number of contributors (which could be the number of taxpayers).

In the early years of pay-as-you-go funding, the system worked well since populations and real incomes were both growing rapidly. Also, women were entering the labour force and thus increasing the number of contributors. Schemes were expanded to cover new categories, and since people contribute before they draw benefits, this expansion was temporarily advantageous. With the cessation of growth, however, social insurance schemes become more expensive (Keyfitz 1984a, 3).

The first indication of funding problems occurred in most countries during the recession of 1981-83. This was not because of any demographic shift, but rather because of increased rates of unemployment. In countries where unemployment insurance is part of the social security system, the recession had a double effect, since unemployment insurance benefits increased at the same time as the number of contributors (or taxpayers) decreased. Even in countries like the United States, where unemployment insurance is separate from the social security system, it has been estimated that every time unemployment rises by one percent their Old Age Security System (OASDI) loses $2 billion a year in revenue (Tamburi 1983, 315).

Also during periods of rising unemployment more workers accept early retirement or disability benefits (if they qualify) provided by the social security system (Tamburi 1983, 315).

In spite of serious financial problems, it should not be overlooked that this period was also characterized by a surprising degree of stability of social security institutions. While there were in certain countries very real attempts to dismantle social security schemes or to make substantial reductions in benefit rights, these were for the most part unsuccessful. On the contrary, developments in certain countries bear witness to the recognition by governments of the importance of social security protection, particularly during times of economic difficulties, as well as strong attachment of the population to the existing social security programmes (International Social Security Association 1983a, 1).

When the economy is weak, it is difficult to raise contribution rates, but some countries reduced benefit payments, which often took the form of delayed or missed benefit increases associated with expected inflation adjustments. Other countries moved to cap benefits or to limit benefits paid to those who are relatively well-off (*e.g.*, the United States made part of the OASDI benefit taxable income for the first time). Other countries supplemented the funding from general tax revenues. In general, however, the long-range problem of the effect of population aging has yet to be addressed.

As to benefits, Table 8.6 shows the maximum benefits available from the plans in five Western industrialized nations (AIW = Average Industrial Wage).

TABLE 8.6

MAXIMUM BENEFIT AVAILABLE

Canada	40% of AIW (C/QPP + OAS)
France	50% of earnings, up to 150% of the AIW
Japan	75% of earnings up to 150% of the AIW
United Kingdom	40% of earnings up to 200% of the AIW
USA	41% of earnings up to 250% of the AIW

SOURCE: The Task Force on Inflation Protection, Vol. 2 1988, 253-326.

Generally speaking, the replacement level in Canada is at the low end of the range presented. Further, for all the countries listed, the amount of eligible earnings upon which benefits are based is greater than in Canada. As a result, in total, Canada's social security retirement benefits are the smallest of the five countries listed.

For a more detailed discussion see Myers 1985b, 955-93; or The Task Force on Inflation Protection, Vol. 2, 253-326.

8.6 CONCLUSIONS

Government-sponsored social security is the basis of economic security for the elderly in Canada. OAS and GIS guarantee a basic floor of income. C/QPP is an important part of guaranteeing a consistent standard of living. As long as the Canadian workforce continued to expand, either through increased births or through increased labour force participation, the pay-as-you-go funding basis of government-sponsored social security systems was attained with relatively low contribution rates. However, with the drop of the birth rate in the 1960s and the resulting aging of the Canadian population, future funding of Canadian social security requires increased contributions or modified benefits. Because Canada has one of the fastest aging populations in the Western world (see Table 2.3), it can anticipate a more rapid rise in costs than other industrialized nations.

Section 6.5 noted that Canadians reported more faith in their own ability to plan for retirement than in government-sponsored plans (Allenvest Group Limited 1985). It is perhaps fortuitous that at a time when the government has limited ability to expand the social security base, Canadians are willing to take more control of their own retirement planning. The proposed expansion of RRSP plans (see Section 6.5) is consistent with this reality. Thus, it appears that Canadian workers will achieve a higher degree of perceived economic security through self-controlled vehicles, such as RRSPs than through government-sponsored social security.

To retain both the reality and perception of economic security, the government must address the public policy issues presented in this chapter and formulate policy that will result in a social security system that will prove to be affordable to the next generation of taxpayers.

CHAPTER 9

SUMMARY OF
PUBLIC POLICY ISSUES

This monograph, through a review of the existing literature, has presented an analysis of the methods available to Canadians to achieve economic security. As noted in Chapter 1, because economic security is a "state of mind or sense of well being... " the perception of security is as important as the reality itself. Thus, to provide a society with economic security, one must not only provide the economic framework, one must also convincingly communicate that the framework is, in fact, secure.

Canada has provided a three-tiered framework for income security for the elderly in that there are three sources of retirement income: the government, the employer, and the individual. An integral part of the overall economic security foundation is the universal health care system.

Canadians are now being promised and are told to expect economic security even with population aging. Questions arise, however, as to whether that promise is either achievable or believed by the populace.

Different chapters presented concerns about many of the parameters that are a key to the Canadian economic security system as now designed. Section 2.5 noted that women are an important source of care provision for the elderly. Concern was raised, however, as to the effect of increased female labour force participation and the expectation of a continuation of this "free" care service. While research has noted no decline in caregiving to date, this needs to be carefully monitored. A reduction in this provision of care would have serious cost implications for the health care system.

Chapter 4 defined the government-sponsored retirement-income security schemes. Because these schemes (including the C/QPP) are funded on a pay-as-you-go basis, their costs will rise rapidly with population aging. The benefits of these programs are not contractually guaranteed. Each generation of workers contributes to pay for the existing retirees in the hope that the next generation will do the same. However, the government can change any of the systems in any manner acceptable to the voters. Evidence of this ability is the recent legislation that will tax-back the OAS benefit from retirees earning more than $50,000 per annum, thus changing OAS to a second tier of the GIS system (see Section 4.8).

Chapter 5 described the present employer-sponsored pension schemes, the second leg of the income-support system. Because such plans are fully funded, their security is not endangered by population aging. Historically, private pensions have left many Canadians without benefits, especially women. However, with pension reform and the continued increase of female labour force participation rates, a much higher proportion of Canadians will achieve significant benefits from employer-sponsored pensions. Thus, this source of economic security is expected to take on increased importance for retirees in the next century. This should mean that fewer Canadians will be dependent upon government-sponsored schemes, especially the GIS.

Both pension reform and tax reform will enhance the role to be played by RRSPs in the provision of retirement income security (Chapter 6). It is not surprising that the government has moved to expand the RRSP sector at a time when opinion polls show that Canadians want more control of their retirement savings schemes and when population aging makes any new government initiatives in income security, or even the expansion of existing plans, cost prohibitive. RRSPs may become the largest source of retirement income security for Canadians in the next century.

Chapter 7 presented government-funded health care as being an integral part of a full economic security model. However, the ability of the government to contain costs in the health care sector (which continue to rise faster than inflation or GNP) has created insecurity in the minds of the taxpayer about the future affordability of health care, especially given that population aging will add to the upward pressure on health care costs.

It was argued that it is the inefficiency of the health care delivery system that must be attacked if costs are to be contained. Alternatives do exist, however, that can be put in place to create a more efficient delivery mechanism. This, in turn, would bring costs under control and put to rest any perception of lack of affordability, given population aging. That assurance would be an added source of security to all Canadians that the cost of their health care system will not jeopardize the security of the entire economic security package.

Chapter 8 discussed social security funding issues and analysed the future impact of funding variables, given the significant increase in costs associated with population aging. While the discussion centred on the funding of government-sponsored social security, the arguments apply to the entire economic security system, including health care, as population aging affects the cost of both systems at the same time (see Figure 9.1). It was argued that the demographic variables of fertility and immigration will not provide a solution to the funding problems.

With a level of future economic growth consistent with past performance, retirement income security need not consume any higher proportion of the GNP pie than it does today. At the same time, population aging means that it will be almost impossible for the government to expand any

FIGURE 9.1

EFFECTS OF AGING POPULATION ON SOCIAL SECURITY AND HEALTH CARE

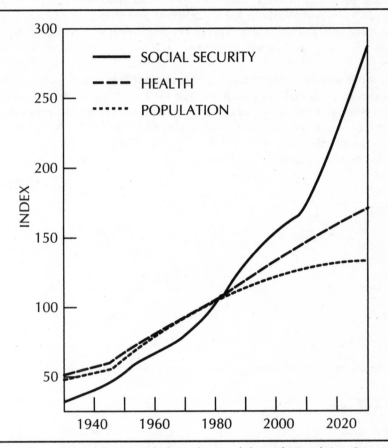

SOURCE: Brown (1988, 58). The graph shows the rate of change for Population, Government Sponsored Social Security, and Government Sponsored Health Care, with 1980 = 100 for all three.

of its existing programs or introduce any new social programs for almost fifty years. Further, there will be little to no opportunity to use enhanced government revenues from economic growth to solve the growing deficit problem.

A final alternative was presented that is being considered in many nations facing the problems associated with population aging; namely, to raise the age of eligibility for government-sponsored retirement income security. It was shown that by raising the age of eligibility from age 65 in 2006 to age 69 in 2030, the Expenditure Dependency Ratio (see Section 8.2) of the years 2000 to 2006 could be held constant. This would mean that population aging would have no impact on the taxpayer. Those wishing to retire early could still do so, but would be required to fund their income-security program through their employer and their own plans. If this resulted in increased labour force participation rates, it would do so at a time when the labour force is expected to decline rapidly so would not be expected to have any negative impacts such as increased unemployment rates.

In summary, this monograph indicates that important public policy issues will be created by population aging. However, it goes on to argue that these issues all have solutions that are attainable and politically palatable. What is necessary is the political will to face these issues and communicate clearly and at the earliest moment the policy alternatives. Only then can true economic security be attained.

GLOSSARY OF TERMS

Canada Pension Plan (CPP) A mandatory earnings-related pension plan administered by the federal government and financed by employee and employer contributions. The CPP guarantees a retirement pension at age 65 equal to 25 percent of a member's adjusted average lifetime earnings, up to a ceiling. The ceiling is based on the year's maximum pensionable earnings (YMPE), which is approximately equal to the Average Industrial Wage. The CPP also provides a disability pension, disabled contributor's child benefit, survivor's pension, orphan's benefit and a lump-sum death benefit. The CPP covers workers outside Quebec; in Quebec, the Quebec Pension Plan provides parallel coverage.

Consumer Price Index Statistics Canada prices a defined list of consumer items such as food and housing on a monthly basis. The Consumer Price Index reflects changes in the cost of this selection of goods.

Defined benefit plan A pension plan that provides a pension whose amount is determined by a defined formula that relates the pension to the employee's number of years of service and, in some plans, to some measure of average or recent levels of pay. An example is a final average plan in which the annual pension is equal to the number of years of service, up to 35, multiplied by 2 percent of the employee's average salary over the last five years of service (*i.e.*, a maximum pension of 70 percent of average salary over the last five years of service).

Defined contribution plan A pension plan where the pension is determined by the amount of annuity that the accumulated contributions plus interest can purchase at retirement. Contributions are normally fixed as a percentage of the employee's salary and may be made by the employee and employer or by the employer alone. These are often called "money purchase plans" (*e.g.*, RRSPs).

Fertility rate The total fertility rate is the number of births that a woman would have in her lifetime if, at each year of age, she experienced the birth rates occurring in the specified calendar year. The fertility rate is an annual (or percentage) measure, even though it is expressed as a hypothetical lifetime (or cohort) measure.

Fully funded A pension plan that at any particular time has sufficient assets to provide for the payment of all pension and other benefits presently earned by current and past members.

Guaranteed Income Supplement (GIS) A federal income security program for the low-income aged. Benefits are indexed quarterly to the Consumer Price Index and paid on a monthly basis. The maximum benefit is reduced by 50 cents for every dollar of other income (other than Old Age Security benefits).

Indexed Pension and life annuity benefits are often adjusted in value to reflect increases in some defined outside index, such as the Consumer Price Index.

Inflation A general and widely diffused increase in the level of prices for various goods and services. The result is a loss in the purchasing power of money, customarily measured by various price indexes (*e.g.*, the Consumer Price Index). Inflation hurts those whose incomes do not rise as fast as prices increase: people with fixed or slowly rising income and savers who lend money. A rise in the index of prices means that it will take more money to buy the same amount of goods and services.

Integrated plan: A plan where benefits and contributions are designed with a view to the total after consideration of the Canada Pension Plan (rarely Old Age Security). For instance, employee contributions might be 5 percent of earnings less CPP contributions, and the benefit may be 2 percent of final salary per year of service, reduced by the amount of CPP benefit assigned to that year of service.

Joint and survivor provision A provision in a pension plan that reduces a member's retirement pension in order to provide a survivor benefit for his or her spouse.

Life annuity A series of periodic payments (usually monthly) payable as long as the policyholder lives.

Life expectancy A statistical measure of the average number of years persons at a given age in a given year can be expected to live under the conditions prevailing in that year.

Locking in A requirement that an employee's and the employer's contributions on his behalf made to a pension plan after a certain date cannot be forfeited or paid as a cash withdrawal if the employee, on termination of employment, has reached a certain age and/or has completed a certain number of years of either service or of plan membership.

Money-purchase plan See defined contribution plan.

Old Age Security (OAS) The basic federal income security program for all

Canadians 65 or older. The monthly benefit is taxable but is not included as income for purposes of computing GIS benefits. Benefits are indexed quarterly to the rise in the Consumer Price Index. For those earning in excess of $50,000, future OAS benefits will be taxed-back in full.

Pay-as-you-go A pension plan which collects just enough money each year through contributions to cover administration costs and current pension benefits.

Pension A fixed dollar amount that is paid regularly over time by a retirement plan, a former employer, or the government to a retired, disabled, or deserving person (or his or her dependents). The amount may be increased partially or fully in later years to compensate for inflation.

Portability Arrangements for the transfer of a member's pension credits either to another pension plan or to a Registered Pension Account when the member changes jobs.

Public pension plans Old Age Security, Guaranteed Income Supplement, Spouse's Allowance, provincial income supplements for the aged, the Canada and Quebec Pension Plans.

Quebec Pension Plan (QPP) A mandatory earnings-related pension plan administered by the Quebec government. The QPP and CPP are basically the same in design.

Registered Pension Plan (RPP) An employer-sponsored pension plan that has been accepted for registration (thereby qualifying for tax assistance) under the *Income Tax Act*.

Registered Retirement Savings Plan (RRSP) An individual retirement savings vehicle provided under the *Income Tax Act*. Taxes are deferred on the contributions and the interest income they earn until the savings are withdrawn, usually as a retirement annuity. Contributions are tax-deductible up to a specified limit.

Replacement ratio The ratio of retirement income to pre-retirement income. The definition (or measure) of both numerator and denominator varies. One of the most important measures is the ratio of *pension* income to pre-retirement earnings. Pension income is typically measured at the "normal retirement age" or at the time of initial start-up of the pension. Earnings are typically an average of the years just before retirement — last three years, high five of the last ten, etc.

Spouse's Allowance (SPA) A federal income security program for couples, one of whose members is receiving GIS and whose other member (the Spouse's Allowance recipient) is aged 60 to 64. A recipient whose spouse died can continue receiving the Spouse's Allowance until he or she reaches 65. Maximum SPA benefits are the sum of an OAS pension and maximum

GIS at the married rate. Like OAS and GIS, SPA is paid monthly and benefits are indexed quarterly.

Survivor benefits Benefits paid to the beneficiary (typically a spouse) of a pension plan member who dies. This benefit is generally equal to 50 or 60 percent of the pension accrued at the time of the member's death.

Vesting The member's right, on termination of employment before retirement under a pension plan, to all or part of the benefit that has accrued under the normal benefit formula of a defined benefit plan, or to the accumulated contributions held on his behalf in a defined contribution plan, up to the date of termination of employment. In simple terms, the pension plan member is entitled to his employer's as well as his own contributions when he leaves his employer. The benefit is often payable as a deferred pension upon retirement.

Year's Basic Exemption (YBE) C/QPP contributors do not pay contributions on earnings below this level, which is 10 percent of the YMPE.

Year's Maximum Pensionable Earnings (YMPE) The maximum earnings for contribution and benefit purposes under the C/QPP.

BIBLIOGRAPHY

Aisenberg, Linda
1987   "Look Who's Got the Cash." *Small Business* October.
Allenvest Group Limited
1985   *Pensions: Perceptions and Proposals.* A Gallup Poll. February.
Asimakopulos, A.
1984   "Financing Canada's Public Pensions — Who Pays?" *Canadian Public Policy* X (2) June.
Auer, L.
1987   *Canadian Hospital Costs and Productivity.* Ottawa: Economic Council of Canada. Ottawa.
Brown, Malcolm C.
1987   *Caring for Profit: Economic Dimensions of Canada's Health Industry.* Vancouver: The Fraser Institute.
Brown, Robert L.
1981   "Let's Pay Homemakers." *Benefits Canada* November/December.
1982   "Actuarial Aspects of the Changing Canadian Demographic Profile." *Transactions of the Society of Actuaries* XXXIV Chicago: 373-97.
1984   "Making Demographics Relevant: The Canadian Baby Boom." *Insurance: Mathematics and Economics* 3.
1987   "Financial Security for the Elderly in Canada." *Proceedings of the Canadian Institute of Actuaries* XVIII. Ottawa.
1988   "The Coming Crisis in Canadian Social Security." *Proceedings, International Congress of Actuaries* 2: 53-68. ICA Helsinki.
Brown, R.L., and F.A. Iglesias
1989   *Social Security Funding Stability: An Age of Eligibility Model.* University of Waterloo, Waterloo: Institute of Insurance and Pension Research, 89-01.
Butz, W.P., and M. Ward
1979   "The emergence of counter-cyclical U.S. Fertility." *American Economic Review* 69 (June): 318-28.

Callahan, Daniel
1987   *Setting Limits: Medical Goals in an Aging Society.* New York: Simon and Shuster.

Calvert, G.N.
1977   *Pensions and Survival* (A *Financial Post* Book) Toronto: Maclean-Hunter.

Canada
1979   Special Senate Committee on Retirement Age Policies. *Retirement Without Tears.* Ottawa: Supply and Services Canada.

1982   *Better Pensions for Canadians.* Ottawa: Ministry of Supply and Services.

1983   *Report of the Parliamentary Task Force on Pension Reform.* Ottawa: Supply and Services Canada.

1986   *Inventory of Income Security Programs in Canada.* Ottawa: Minster of Supply and Services, July 1985.

1988   House of Commons Human Rights Committee. *Human Rights and Aging.* Ottawa: Supply and Services Canada.

Canada, Office of the Superintendent of Financial Institutions.
1988   *Canada Pension Plan, Statutory Actuarial Report No. 11.* As at December 31, 1988. Ottawa.

Canada Pension Plan
Advisory Committee
1984   *A Report on the Funding of the Canada Pension Plan.* Ottawa, October.

Canadian Medical Association
1984   *Health: A Need for Redirection.* A Task Force on the Allocation of Health Care Resources. Ottawa: Action Limited.

Chappell, N.L., L.A. Strain and A.A. Blandford
1986   *Aging and Health Care: A Social Perspective.* Toronto: Holt Rinehart and Winston of Canada, Limited.

Chen, Yung-Ping
1987   "Making Assets out of Tomorrow's Elderly." *The Gerontologist* 27(4): 410-16.

1988   "Better options for Work and Retirement: Some Suggestions for Improving Economic Security Mechanisms for Old Age." *Annual Review of Gerontology and Geriatrics* 8: 189-216.

Connidis, Ingrid Arnet
1989   *Family Ties and Aging.* Toronto: Butterworths.

Coward, L.E.
1988   *Mercer Handbook of Canadian Pension and Welfare Plans,* (9th ed.). Don Mills: CCH Canadian Ltd.

Delaney, T.
1987   *The Delaney Report on R.R.S.P.'s* 1988 Edition. Toronto: McGraw Hill Ryerson.

Denton, F.T., M.L. Kliman and B.G. Spencer
  1981   *Pensions and the Economic Security of the Elderly.* Hamilton: C.D. Howe Institute.
Denton, F.T., C.H. Feaver, and B.G. Spencer
  1986   "Prospective Aging of the Population and Its Implications for the Labour Force and Government Expenditure." *Canadian Journal on Aging* 5(2): 75-98.
Denton, F.T., and B.G. Spencer
  1984a   *Population Aging and the Economy: Some Issues in Resource Allocation.* QSEP Research Report No. 105. McMaster University: Program for Quantitative Studies in Economics and Population, 1984-18
  1984b   *Prospective Changes in the Population and Their Implications for Government Expenditure.* QSEP Research Report No. 98 (June). McMaster University: Program for Quantitative Studies in Economics and Population.
  1987   *Population Change and The Future Labour Force: A Discussion Paper.* QSEP Research Report No. 187 (January). McMaster University: Program for Quantitative Studies in Economics and Population.
Department of International Economic and Social Affairs
  1984   *Bulletin on Aging* IX (3). United Nations.
Easterlin, Richard A.
  1978   "What will 1984 Be Like? Socioeconomic Implications of Recent Twists in Age Structure." *Demography* 15(4): 397-432.
  1984   *Bulletin on Aging* IX (3). United Nations.
  1987   *Birth and Fortune, the Impact of Numbers on Personal Welfare.* London: Grant McIntyre.
Economic Council of Canada
  1979   *One in Three — Pensions for Canadians to 2030.* Ottawa.
  1987a   *au courant* 4,(1). Ottawa.
  1987b   *Aging with Limited Health Resources.* Proceedings of a Colloquium on Health Care, Ottawa. May 1986.
Ermisch, John F.
  1983   *The Political Economy of Demographic Change.* Policy Studies Institute. London: Heinemann Books.
Evans, R.G.
  1976   "Does Canada Have Too Many Doctors? Why Nobody Loves an Immigrant Physician." *Canadian Public Policy* 2: 147-60.
  1984   *Strained Mercy: The Economics of Canadian Health Care.* Toronto: Butterworths.
  1987   "Hang Together or Hang Separately: The Viability of a Universal Health Care System in an Aging Society." *Canadian Public Policy* XIII (2): 165-80.

Fellegi, Ivan P.
  1988   "Can We Afford an Aging Society?" *Canadian Economic Observer* (October) Ottawa: Statistics Canada.
Fisher, R.M., and M.L. Zorzitto
  1983   "Placement Problem: Diagnosis Disease or Term of Denigration?" *Canadian Medical Association Journal* 129 (August 15): 331-34.
Foot, David K.
  1982   *Canada's Population Outlook, Demographic Futures and Economic Challenges.* Canadian Institute for Economic Policy, Toronto: Lorimer.
———, and Daniel Trefler
  1983   *Life-cycle Saving and Population Aging.* No. 8308 (March). Working Paper Series. Institute for Policy Analysis. University of Toronto.
Forbes, W.F., J.A. Jackson and A.S. Kraus
  1987   *Institutionalization of the Elderly in Canada.* Toronto: Butterworths.
Gee, Ellen M. and Meredith M. Kimball
  1987   *Women and Aging.* Toronto: Butterworths.
Gross, J., and G.W. Schwenger
  1981   *Health Care Costs for the Elderly in Ontario: 1976-2026.* Toronto: Ontario Economic Council.
Health and Welfare Canada
  1982   *Better Pensions for Canadians.* Ottawa: Minister of Supply and Services.
  1984   *Income Security Programs.* Ottawa: Minister of Supply and Services, October.
  1985   *Income Security Programs.* Research Note 7. Ottawa: Ministry of Supply and Services, June.
  1987a   *Basic Facts on Social Security Programs.* Ottawa: Ministry of Supply and Services, March.
  1987b   *Posing the Questions: Review of Demography and Its Implications for Economics and Social Policy.* Ottawa: Ministry of Supply and Services.
  1987c   *Social Security Statistics, Canada and the Provinces, 1960-61 to 1984-85.* Ottawa: Ministry of Supply and Services, November.
  1989a   *Inventory of Income Security Programs in Canada.* Ottawa: Ministry of Supply and Services, January 1988.
  1989b   *Charting Canada's Future.* A Report of the Demographic Review. Ottawa: Ministry of Supply and Services.
Hewitt Associates.
  1987   *Canada: Pension Increases after Retirement* (also found in the Task Force on Inflation Protection for Employment Pension Plans). Toronto.

Hohn, Charlotte
1987   "Population Policies in Advanced Societies: Pronatalist and Migration Strategies." *European Journal of Population* 3: 459-81.
Iglehart, John K.
1986   "Canada's Health Care System." *New England Journal of Medicine* 315(3): 202-208.
International Labour Office
1984   *Financing Social Security: The Options.* An international analysis. Geneva: International Labour Office.
International Social Security Association
1983a   *Developments in Social Security and ISSA Activities 1981-1983* Report I. XXIst General Assembly. Geneva, October 3-13.
1983b   *Improving Cost Effectiveness in Health Care.* Studies and Research No. 19. Geneva.
1984   *Long-Term Care and Social Security.* Studies and Research No. 21. Geneva.
1986   *Developments in Social Security and ISSA Activities 1984-1986.* Reports I, II, III, IV. XXII General Assembly. Montreal, September 2-12.
1987   *Conjugating Public and Private: The Case of Pensions.* Studies and Research No. 24. Geneva.
Japan Foundation for Research and Development of Pension Schemes,
1986   *National System of Old-Age and Disability and Survivors' Benefits in Japan* (2nd ed.).
Kane, R.L., and R.A. Kane
1985   "The Feasibility of Universal Long-term Care Benefits: Ideas from Canada." *New England Journal of Medicine* 312: 1357-64.
Kettle, John
1980   *The Big Generation,* Toronto: McClelland and Stewart.
Keyfitz, N., and J.A. Beekman
1984   *Demography Through Problems.* New York: Springer-Verlag.
Keyfitz, Nathan
1984a   *Demographic Aging and Pressures on the Welfare State* (July). Laxenburg, Austria: International Institute for Applied Systems Analysis.
1984b   *The Post-War Rise and Fall in Births and Its Consequences* (July). Laxenburg, Austria: International Institute for Applied Systems Analysis.
1984c   *Some Demographic Properties of Transfer Schemes: How to Achieve Equity Between the Generations* (August). Laxenburg, Austria: International Institute for Applied Systems Analysis.
Kulp, C.A., and J.W. Hall
1968   *Casualty Insurance* (4th ed.) New York: Ronald Press Co.
Longhurst, Patrick, and Rose Marie Earle
1987   *Looking After the Future.* Toronto: Doubleday.

Marr, W., and D. McCready
  1989   *The Effects of Demographic Structure on Consumption and Savings Patterns in Canada.* Ottawa: Institute for Research on Public Policy.
Marshall, Victor W.
  1987   *Aging in Canada, Social Perspectives* (2nd ed.). Markham: Fitzhenry and Whiteside.
McDaniel, Susan A.
  1986   *Canada's Aging Population.* Toronto: Butterworths.
  1987   "Demographic Aging as a Guiding Paradigm in Canada's Welfare State." *Canadian Public Policy* XIII (3): 330-36.
McDonald, Lynn
  1985   "Poverty, Pension and Change". A paper presented to the 14th Annual Scientific and Educational Meeting of the Canadian Association of Gerontology, October 17-20, Hamilton.
——, and Richard Warner
  1990   *Retirement in Canada.* Toronto: Butterworths.
McPherson, Barry
  1983   *Aging as a Social Process: An Introduction to Individual and Population Aging.* Toronto: Butterworths.
Mercer's Bulletin,
  1988   (May) 38(5). Toronto.
Myers, Robert J.
  1985a   "Implications of Population Change on Social Insurance Systems Providing Old-age Benefits." *Insurance, Mathematics and Economics* 4(1) (January).
  1985b   *Social Security* (3rd ed.). McCahan Foundations: Richard D. Homewood, Illinois: Richard D. Irwin, Inc.
National Council of Welfare
  1984a   *Sixty-Five and Older* (February). Ottawa.
  1984b   *A Pension Primer* (April). Ottawa.
  1984c   *Pension Reform* (May). Ottawa.
  1988   *Poverty Profile* (April). Ottawa.
  1989a   *The 1989 Budget and Social Policy* (September). Ottawa.
  1989b   *A Pension Primer* (September). Ottawa.
  1990   *Pension Reform* (February). Ottawa.
Nowak, Mark
  1988   *Aging and Society: A Canadian Perspective.* Toronto: Nelson Canada.
Ontario Economic Council
  1983   *Pensions Today and Tomorrow.* Toronto.
Ontario Select Committee on Pensions
  1982   *Final Report.* Ontario Legislative Assembly. Toronto.

Ontario Task Force on Mandatory Retirement
1987   *Fairness and Flexibility in Retiring from Work* (December). Toronto.
Perron, Pierre
1987   *Macroeconomics and the Canadian Income-Security System: An Overview.* (September). Discussion Paper No. 336 Ottawa: Economic Council of Canada.
Pifer, Alan, and Lydia Bronte
1986   *Our Aging Society: Paradox and Promise* New York: W.W. Norton and Company.
Preston, Samuel H.
1984   "Children and the Elderly in the U.S." *Scientific American* (December), 44-49.
Price, Waterhouse, - Medicus
1988   *Direct Nursing Care Requirements of Extended Care Residents in Homes for the Aged and Nursing Homes in Ontario* (March). Toronto.
Province of Ontario
1983   *Health Care: The 80's and Beyond, Seeking Consensus.* Toronto: Queen's Printer for Ontario.
1984   *Proposals for Pension Reform.* Toronto: Queen's Printer for Ontario.
1987   *Toward a Shared Direction for Health in Ontario.* Report of the Ontario Health Review Panel. Toronto: Queen's Printer for Ontario.
Quebec
1986   *Actuarial Report of the Quebec Pension Plan* (December 31).
Rejda, G.E.
1988   *Social Insurance and Economic Security* (3rd ed.). Englewood Cliffs, N.J.: Prentice-Hall.
Rhee, H.A.
1974   *Human Ageing and Retirement.* Geneva: International Society Security Association.
Revenue Canada
1989   *Taxation Statistics for 1987.* Ottawa: Ministry of Supply and Services Canada.
Rosa, Jean-Jacques
1982   *The World Crisis in Social Security.* California: Foundation Nationale d'economie politique and Institute for Contemporary Studies.
Royal Commission on the Status of Pensions in Ontario
1981   *Summary Report.* Government of Ontario. Toronto: Queen's Printer for Ontario.

Schulz, James H.
  1985   *The Economics of Aging* (3rd ed.). Belmont, California: Wadsworth Publishing Co.
Seward, Shirley B.
  1987   *Canadian Economy: An Overview* (January). Ottawa: The Institute for Research on Public Policy.
Simmons-Tropea, D., R.W. Osborn, and C.W. Schwenger
  1986   *Health Status and Health Services for Elderly Canadians.* Research Paper No. 8, Programme in Gerontology. University of Toronto.
Soderstrom, L.
  1982   "The Life-Cycle Hypothesis and Aggregate Household Saving." *American Economic Review* 72 (June): 590-96.
Statistics Canada
  1982   *Census of Canada 1981 Population* (Catalogue 92-901). Ottawa: Ministry of Supply and Services.
  1984a   *Pension Plans in Canada, 1982* (Catalogue 74-104). Ottawa: Ministry of Supply and Services.
  1984b   *Life Tables 1980-82, Canada and Provinces* (Catalogue 84-532). Ottawa: Ministry of Supply and Services.
  1984c   *Family Expenditures in Canada* (Catalogue 62-555). Ottawa: Ministry of Supply and Services.
  1984d   *Current Demographic Analysis, Fertility in Canada* (Catalogue 91-524E). Ottawa: Ministry of Supply and Services.
  1986a   *Household Facilities by Income and Other Characteristics, 1985.* (Catalogue No. 13-567). Ottawa: Ministry of Supply and Services.
  1986b   *Current Demographic Analysis: Report on the Demographic Situation in Canada* (Catalogue 91-209E). Ottawa: Ministry of Supply and Services.
  1988a   *Historical Labour Force Statistics* (Catalogue 71-201). Ottawa: Ministry of Supply and Services.
  1988b   *Pensions and Income of the Elderly in Canada* (Catalogue No. 13-588(2)). Ottawa: Ministry of Supply and Services.
  1989a   *Hospital Morbidity* (Catalogue No. 82-206). Ottawa: Ministry of Supply and Services.
  1989b   *Life Tables, Canada and Provinces, 1985-87* (Catalogue 84-532). Ottawa: Ministry of Supply and Services.
Statistics Canada
(Nagnur, Dhruva)
  1986   *Longevity and Historical Life Tables 1921-1981 (Abridged), Canada and the Provinces.* Ottawa: Ministry of Supply and Services.
Tamburi, G.
  1983   "Escalation of State Pension Costs: The Reasons and the Issues." *International Labour Review* 122(3).

Task Force on Inflation
Protection for Employment
Pension Plans
    1988   *Report*. Toronto: Queen's Printer for Ontario. Vol. 1, *Research Studies*. Vol. 2, *Research Studies*.
The Financial Post
    1988   "Annual Money Planner." (Winter). *Moneywize Magazine*.
Townson, Monica
    1988   "Indexing to Inflation: What Steps are Being Taken?" *The Financial Post Moneywize Magazine* (May).
Treasurer of Ontario
    1984   *Ontario Proposals for Pension Reform* (April) Toronto: Queen's Printer for Ontario.
United Nations
    1984   *Bulletin on Aging* IX: 3. Dept. of International Economic and Social Affairs.
United States Department of Health and Human Services
    1985   *Social Security Programs Throughout the World*. Social Security Administration Research Report #60. Washington.
United States Department of Commerce
    1987   *An Aging World: International Population Report Series* P-95:78 (September). Washington: Bureau of the Census.
Vaupel, J., and A. Yashin
    1983   *The Deviant Dynamics of Death in Heterogeneous Populations*. Laxenburg, Austria: International Institute for Applied Systems Analysis.
Weitz, Harry
    1979   *The Foreign Experience with Income Maintenance for the Elderly*. Ottawa: Economic Council of Canada.
Wigdor, Blossom T., and David K. Foot
    1988   *The Over-Forty Society*. Toronto: James Lorimer & Company.

INDEX